JOURNALISM AND
THE NSA REVELATIONS

The Reuters Institute for the Study of Journalism at the University of Oxford aims to serve as the leading international forum for a productive engagement between scholars from a wide range of disciplines and practitioners of journalism. As part of this mission, we publish work by academics, journalists, and media industry professionals focusing on some of the most important issues facing journalism around the world today.

All our books are reviewed by both our Editorial Committee and expert readers. Our books, however, remain the work of authors writing in their individual capacities, not a collective expression of views from the Institute.

JOURNALISM AND THE NSA REVELATIONS

PRIVACY, SECURITY AND THE PRESS

EDITED BY RISTO KUNELIUS, HEIKKI HEIKKILÄ, ADRIENNE RUSSELL AND DMITRY YAGODIN

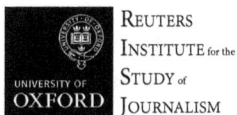

REUTERS
INSTITUTE for the
STUDY of
JOURNALISM

UNIVERSITY OF
OXFORD

I.B. TAURIS
LONDON · NEW YORK

Published by I.B.Tauris & Co. Ltd in association with
the Reuters Institute for the Study of Journalism, University of Oxford

Published in 2017 by
I.B.Tauris & Co. Ltd
London • New York
www.ibtauris.com

ISBN (HB): 978 1 78453 675 6
ISBN (PB): 978 1 78453 676 3
eISBN: 978 1 78672 189 1
ePDF: 978 1 78673 189 0

A full CIP record for this book is available from the British Library
A full CIP record is available from the Library of Congress

Library of Congress Catalog Card Number: available

Typeset by Riverside Publishing Solutions, Salisbury, SP4 6NQ

Contents

Tables and Figures

Tables

Figures

Contributors

Olivier Baisnée is Associate Professor of Political Science at Sciences Po Toulouse. His research interests include EU news, EU correspondence, coverage of protests and the history of the French journalistic field.

Elisabeth Eide is Professor of Journalism Studies at Oslo and Akershus University College of Applied Sciences, Norway. She has led several research projects, and has written, edited and co-edited a number of books on transnational media events, climate change and journalism, as well as five novels.

Ruolin Fang is an MA student at the School of Government in Sun Yat-sen University, China.

Heikki Heikkilä is Senior Researcher at the Faculty of Communication, University of Tampere, Finland. His research interests relate to digital journalism, audience studies, media accountability, and theories of the public sphere and privacy. He has published more than 20 journal articles and book chapters in international publications.

Katy Jones is a lecturer in language and communication at Cardiff University. Her research interests include approaching the study of language (in particular referring expressions) from an integrated perspective, combining areas such as discourse analysis, cognitive linguistics, pragmatics, and functional grammar. She is the co-author of *Referring in Language: An Integrated Approach* (forthcoming).

Risto Kunelius is Professor of Journalism at the Faculty of Communication, University of Tampere, Finland. His current research interests include media and power, mediatisation and social theory, climate change, and journalism. His recent work has been published in *Communication Theory*,

Digital Journalism, and *International Journal of Press/Politics.* He is the co-editor and author of *Media and Global Climate Knowledge: Journalism and the IPCC* (with Elisabeth Eide, Dmitry Yagodin, and Matt Tegelberg, 2017).

Dennis Leung is a PhD candidate at the School of Journalism and Communication, Chinese University of Hong Kong.

Anne Mollen is a PhD student at the Centre for Media, Communication and Information Research at the University of Bremen. She is co-author of *The Communicative Construction of Europe* (2015). Her research interests include digital media technologies, social media practices, and civic online communication.

Johanna Möller is a postdoctoral researcher at the Department of Communication at the Johannes Gutenberg-University Mainz. Her recently published doctoral thesis looks at transcultural public actors in the field of Polish–German political communication. She is co-author of two monographs on the Europeanisation of public spheres. Her current research focuses on shifts in the realm of the political in an age of digital information and communication technologies.

Frédéric Nicolas is a PhD student in sociology at the National Institute for Agronomic Research (University of Burgundy, France) and at the Laboratoire des Sciences Sociales du Politique (Toulouse School of Political Science). His current research interests include the sociology of media, political sociology, and the sociology of work. He is also an assistant professor at the University of Limoges.

Adrienne Russell is Associate Professor and Graduate Director in the Media, Film and Journalism Studies department, University of Denver. She is the author of *Networked: A Contemporary History of News in Transition* (2011) and *Journalism as Activism: Recoding Media Power* (2016).

Karin Wahl-Jorgensen is a professor in the Cardiff School of Journalism, Media and Cultural Studies, where she also serves as Director of Research Development and Environment. Her research focuses on journalism and citizenship. She has written some 50 journal articles and 30 book chapters, and authored or edited five books. Recent books include *Emotions, Media and Politics* (forthcoming), *Disasters and the Media* (2012, with Mervi Pantti and Simon Cottle), and the *Handbook of Journalism Studies* (2009, co-edited with Thomas Hanitzsch).

Silvio Waisbord is a professor in the School of Media and Public Affairs at George Washington University. He is editor-in-chief of the *Journal of Communication* and former editor-in-chief of the *International Journal of Press/Politics*. His recent books include *Media Movements: Civil Society and Media Policy Reform in Latin America* (with María Soledad Segura, 2016), and the co-edited volumes *Routledge Companion to Media and Human Rights* (with Howard Tumber, 2017), and *News of Baltimore: Race, Rage and the City* (with Linda Steiner, 2017).

Haiyan Wang is Associate Professor in the School of Communication and Design at Sun Yat-sen University, China. Her recent publications have appeared in *Media Culture and Society, Journalism, International Journal of Communication, Asian Journal of Communication, China Review, Global Media and China, Journalism Practice*, and a number of renowned Chinese-language journals. She is author of *The Transformation of Investigative Journalism in China: From Journalists to Activists* (2016).

Dmitry Yagodin is a postdoctoral researcher at the Faculty of Communication, University of Tampere, Finland. His research interests lie in the areas of strategic communication, alternative media practices, and digital media cultures.

Acknowledgements

This book has been in the works almost as long as Edward Snowden has been in exile. Throughout the process of researching and writing, we have greatly benefited from the generous support of a long list of people and institutions.

The Finnish Helsingin Sanomat Foundation is an exceptional backer of international research and reflection on the role of journalism in the changing world. Thanks to past and current presidents Heleena Savela and Ulla Koski, whose support of the project has been both steady and flexible. Thank you for skilled editorial guidance to Rasmus Kleis Nielsen and Alex Reid at the University of Oxford's Reuters Institute for the Study of Journalism, and also to the Institute's editorial board and reviewers. Thank you to Sara Magness at I.B.Tauris for making the final stretch of production smooth. And we are grateful to the Tampere Research Centre for Journalism, Media and Communication (COMET), the home base of this project, for the skill of Heli Heino and the patient support of the its research directors Pentti Raittila and Katja Valaskivi.

During the research, reflection and writing, a wide network of colleagues have offered invaluable expertise. Nick Couldry and Damian Tambini in London and Andreas Hepp in Bremen were crucial to getting the project off the ground. Arne Hintz and the broader Cardiff University 'Digital Citizenship and Surveillance Society' research group offered input and advice throughout the project. Thanks to John Tomasic and Matt Tegelberg for talented language editing. Jennifer Filipetti in Boulder and Jeremy Deaton in Washington were instrumental in the US analysis. And, of course, we are grateful for the commitment of all authors in the book.

Finally, our collective gratitude also goes out to all of those involved in bringing the Snowden revelations to light. In particular, we wish to thank Ben Wizner and Alan Rusbridger, who shared their insights with us at a crucial stage of writing this book. Their work on behalf of the public interest is an inspiration.

**Risto Kunelius, Heikki Heikkilä,
Adrienne Russell, Dmitry Yagodin**

1

The NSA Revelations as a Prism

*Risto Kunelius, Heikki Heikkilä, Adrienne Russell,
and Elisabeth Eide*

The story of Edward Snowden, the National Security Agency (NSA),
and US government global surveillance operations has been told many
times and in many ways – in news articles and television spots, in
documentary films, investigative books, academic works, as the subject of
popular culture products and web-hosted 'live chats'. In the public eye,
it began on 5 June 2013, when the *Guardian* ran a piece by Glenn
Greenwald and Ewen MacAskill, which revealed the fact that major
telecommunications company Verizon had been forced by the
government to provide the NSA with access to the phone records of
millions of Americans. On the following day, Barton Gellman and Laura
Poitras published an exposé in the *Washington Post* in which they reported
that the NSA had collected private digital information from major
companies through a programme code-named PRISM. The stories were
the first drops in a downpour of revelations about secret government
programmes designed around mass surveillance or systematic snooping
and spying.

Reactions to the leaked information issued from political, legal,
and social institutions around the world. The name of the notorious
programme singled out in the *Washington Post* exposé became an
appropriate metaphor for an unfolding media event: the leaks worked like
a ray of light passing through the prism of public discourse, raising
disturbing questions about the trade-offs and tensions between security
and privacy.

On 7 June, Snowden appeared in a video, first posted on the *Guardian*
website and later circulated on news and social media platforms across the
web. In the 12-minute interview, he described the scope and pervasiveness
of digital surveillance, and asked for the public – rather than the

intelligence community or obscure secret courts – to determine whether or not the following practice is legitimate.

The NSA specifically targets the communications of everyone. It ingests them by default. It collects them in its systems, it filters them, it analyses them, it measures them, it stores them for periods of time simply because that is the easiest, most efficient, and most valuable means to achieve these ends. ... Any analyst at any time can target anyone. ... Not all analysts have the ability to target everything, but I sitting at my desk certainly had the authority to wiretap anyone from you or your accountant to a federal judge or even the President. (Guardian, 11 June 2013)[1]

The initial revelations set in motion an unfolding event that garnered massive media attention around the world.[2] Consecutive scoops drawn from the Snowden files published in several news outlets kept the case close to the heart of the international news agenda. Towards the end of 2014, the high peak of media attention had passed, but the issue had become a sustained news topic and Snowden a routine cast member of the global debate on security, privacy, and surveillance. At the same time, the NSA had become the subject of constant online inquiry and had been introduced into people's everyday vocabulary.

As Snowden stepped into the spotlight, the narrative gained momentum, but it also split into two. On the one hand, the story inevitably became about him: his motives, background, and movements from Hong Kong to the Sheremetyevo airport outside Moscow and to his 'temporary' asylum in Russia. A stream of interviews, more video appearances, some public smearing, and occasional moments of international public recognition added new chapters to the story. As a result, many people see Snowden as a traitor; many others see him as a heroic spokesman for transparency and the public's right to know.

The line between noble whistle-blowers and irresponsible leakers has always been fraught. It is not surprising that Snowden, too, is the subject of deeply divided opinion, often depending on the political views and vested interests. Nevertheless, whether or not Snowden did the right thing, few would agree that the debate, centred around Snowden – on his motives and the facts he revealed – has been futile or that we would have been better off without having engaged in the debate at all. On the whistle-blowing side, the revelations have been greeted as a major breakthrough, a 'single act of conscience' that 'literally altered the course of history', as Glenn Greenwald (2014: 253) concludes his narrative. On the other side, the former director of both the NSA and the CIA closes his account on the matter with a reflection on the 'peculiar gift' of Snowden: making visible the dilemma between the effectiveness and legitimacy of surveillance that tries to serve national interests (Hayden, 2016: 416, 421–4). Beside their profound disagreements, Greenwald and Hayden tend to agree that the Snowden case raises fundamental questions about the rules and functions of states, political institutions, and businesses in the digital age.

The starting point of this book is that the Snowden revelations and the public debate that followed those revelations provide a unique opportunity to study ways we think about privacy and security and how our views on those topics relate to broader assumptions about society, citizenship, and democracy. The complexity of this debate does not merely stem from the fact that it drew very distinct groups of actors together: heads of state, intelligence experts, politicians, internet company CEOs, civic activists, and everyday internet users. In addition, it is apparent that, given the distinct roles these actors play in society, and its division of labour, they come at the debate with certain perspectives.

In regard to privacy, for instance, intelligence experts tend to emphasise that privacy is historically a nation-based privilege, a secondary value constrained by state security. Whereas for liberal political institutions, privacy is primarily a source of political legitimacy, as the will of the people is supposed to emanate from reflection both public and private, and expressed in the solitude of the election booth. Partly coinciding with this, political activists identify privacy as an essential ingredient in a democracy, as privacy acts to safeguard political pluralism and serves as fuel for dissent and a check on power.

Within the realms of business and consumption, digital privacy gains somewhat different meanings. For internet service providers and digital businesses, privacy is recognised for its value in calculating how to serve up deeply personalised communication and laser-sharp, targeted advertising. This has turned privacy into a commodity to be traded in the market for audiences. For digital everyday living, privacy increasingly becomes a form of currency with which we pay for better services – be they commercial or public. For individuals, privacy also denotes a psychological necessity, a sense of authenticity, of being able to experience the difference between you and everyone else (Heikkilä and Kunelius, 2017).

The way privacy is variously understood (cf. Vincent, 2016) today demonstrates the importance of contextual judgement: what is reasonable and acceptable depends on the situation (Solove, 2011; Nissenbaum, 2010). If, indeed, 'context is all', as Garton Ash (2016: 291) reminds us, the unique context of Snowden's revelations demonstrates that, where information is made digital, all data related to its production, distribution, and consumption can be collected, tracked down, and harnessed for use. Of course, many ways we use private information – in the form of actual contents or metadata – enhance our lives and so are legitimate, as Nick Couldry writes.[3] At the same time, he adds, we should be aware of the fact that data collection facilitates the emergence of practical (political and economic) order and that the power of that order to change our lives are to a great extent unexplored (see also Couldry & Hepp, 2017).

Journalism is intensively implicated in this changing terrain (Lloyd, 2017). This book explores what Snowden's actions and the discourse that has attempted to make sense of the reactions to and repercussions of his actions can tell us about today's journalism and about the political, technological, and cultural environments in which journalism is developing. In exploring public discourse, we can map out some of the dominant reactions to the leaks across the world and pin down plausible consequences for journalism and journalists. Our study focuses on the relationship between journalism and the state. How is journalism drawn into the orbit of national political interests, and in what ways is the autonomy of journalism being addressed and defended? A broader international perspective on the issue leads us to probe the role of domestication and transnationalism in the Snowden debates. Are there nationally distinct debates being waged on surveillance and/or to what extent are transnational principles of justification shaping those debates?

Ambiguity prevails

Snowden's revelations have been more consequential than merely pointing attention to the new material realities of the global digital world. They have had real-world effects. The US government, for instance, has publicly stepped back from some of the surveillance techniques exposed by Snowden as courts ruled them unconstitutional.[4] Still, many members of the security community continue to believe the techniques are effective and necessary – and many journalists largely agree. The responses of journalists to Snowden and the leaks, like those of the public and lawmakers, have been varied, as illustrated by the evidence analysed in this book.

In January 2014, seven months into the controversy, the *New York Times* summarised its position on the moral balance of the case:

> *In retrospect, Mr. Snowden was clearly justified in believing that the only way to blow the whistle on this kind of intelligence-gathering was to expose it to the public and let the resulting furor do the work his superiors would not. … President Obama should tell his aides to begin finding a way to end Mr. Snowden's vilification and give him an incentive to return home.* (New York Times, 1 January 2014)

This assessment of Snowden's actions as justified has been echoed by prestigious civil rights and good government organisations, reflecting a view of Snowden and his collaborators as champions of the public interest and of the most valuable sort of journalism. In 2014, the *Washington Post* and the *Guardian* were awarded Pulitzer Prizes for their coverage of NSA surveillance. That same year Glenn Greenwald, Laura Poitras, Ewen MacAskill, and Barton Gellman, the journalists closest to the story, were awarded the George Polk Award for National Security Reporting. In their acceptance speeches, Poitras and Greenwald also paid tribute to their source: 'Each one of these awards just provides further vindication that what [Snowden] did in coming forward was absolutely the right thing to do and merits gratitude, and not indictments and decades in prison.'[5] Since the revelations, Snowden has also emerged as an active speaker and expert commentator in the global privacy–security debate. He is extremely active and popular on Twitter, attracting 2.7 million followers.

Critics of Snowden – and those who advocate his indictment if he returns to the US – continue to question his motives. They argue that secret national security programmes are not excessive but, rather, necessary and justified, particularly given the ongoing conflict between the West and terrorist groups like Daesh/ISIS or Al-Qaeda. The pervasive threat of terror attacks has provided much support for such arguments. Thus, while posing critical questions concerning the legitimacy of internet surveillance, the leaks have also provided more fodder for calls demanding greater control of the internet. In such views – irrespective of whether these claims are made in the US or in Russia – privacy is essentially seen as a secondary value; something that must ultimately be compromised in the name of security.

In the broad global frame, the NSA leaks are symptomatic of ambiguities in the political landscape resulting from the intersection of security discourses in the aftermath of the 9/11 terrorist attacks, a transparency culture emboldened by the internet, and a multi-polar geopolitical landscape in which many nations are vying for power. It is in this highly charged global political landscape that the Enlightenment notion of 'liberal privacy' is being renegotiated and tested. The debate around Snowden and his revelations, then, is in a sense a test case for political and symbolic power invested in the notion of privacy, in a situation where – as noted above – the material and historical conditions where it was coined (in different constitutional variations) are shifting and challenged. While we recognise that the liberal expectation of privacy can be construed as something fundamental for human life, we also bear in mind that it is a historical – and therefore evolving – achievement.

Media historian John Nerone (2015a) describes grand political conjunctures as 'tests of capacity' for journalism that can shape the profession for the future. As a dramatically intense public event where security, privacy, and civic rights intersect, the NSA case offers a chance to take stock of political and social forces that have a stake in shaping the role of journalism – nationally and globally. The core of journalism as a profession is its ability to sustain some measure of control over its own practices and thus social and political autonomy (Waisbord, 2013). A key aspect of journalism's influence stems from its ability to publicly defend its autonomy in the face of powerful actors and institutions that control other resources of power. The discussion about Snowden, inevitably, becomes a moment when many of these public, symbolic resources are judged and reconsidered. It is indeed the press that Ben Wizner, director of the American Civil Liberties Union's (ACLU) Speech, Privacy and Technology Project (and Snowden's lawyer), credits with the success of the leaks: 'Democratic oversight has been reinvigorated,' he has said, 'but the irony is that it took a dramatic act of law breaking, and a free press willing to defy the demands of the government' (Wizner, 2015a).

In a public letter two years after the leaks (*New York Times*, 4 June 2015), Snowden himself expressed relief that the debate had taken off and hope that it would bring positive change. He admitted being worried that 'the public would react with indifference, or practiced cynicism'. He went on to cite instances of the 'power of an informed public' mobilised for local legal battles, global declarations, as well as developing counter-technologies for the self-protection of internet users. He concluded with decided optimism: 'For the first time since the attacks of Sept. 11, 2001, we see the outline of a politics that turns away from reaction and fear in favor of resilience and reason.'

In June 2015 Snowden was writing in the wake of the passage of the US Freedom Act, which – after a fierce political battle – introduced changes to the US legal framework of surveillance. At the same time, a major review on the 'investigatory powers' by David Anderson in the UK was published. The review suggested new, comprehensive legislation, emphasising the need to build a more coherent and functional framework to govern the interface between surveillance and privacy (Anderson, 2015). Alan Rusbridger summed up the situation:

> I can't imagine a moment at which this ever becomes a settled issue. ... The public is on a vertical learning curve. There are bound to be lots of legal challenges. ... This [case] is a sort of metaphor for the 21st century, in which this particular issue, and the way that it's been brought into the public, dramatises lots of the issues that we're going to have to work out with technology. (Rusbridger, 2015)

The authors of this book view the revelations as a disruptive moment in which debate on these twenty-first-century issues was intensified. The leaks saw the vested interests of stakeholders come more sharply into the public view. This is not to claim that the NSA leaks will prove to be a decisive turning point. It is a claim that the leaks mobilise a considerable amount of transformative potential. The disclosure that resulted from the leaks demands a public working-through of how privacy, security, and surveillance are – or should be – balanced. While traditions of privacy serve as a resource in this debate, privacy itself is an object of this debate.

For journalism, the leaks raise a potentially transformative question, because in Western political discourse, the 'public' and the 'private' are mutually constitutive terms. Surveillance, digital tracking, and sorting highlight an increased inability of people to secure a space in which pluralist critiques of the political system can be safely articulated, let alone calls for limits on securitised politics. With a view towards everyday digital privacy, the leaks have suggested citizens must ultimately choose between exiting the digital world or accepting the life enhancements of the digital world while adopting an attitude of practised cynicism or ironic lightness, as the 'I have nothing to hide' dictum suggests. No wonder opinion polls often suggest that people are simultaneously worried about privacy and aware of their inability to control personal information.

This book tracks the flow of the Snowden–NSA debate in six countries: the United States, the United Kingdom, France, Germany, China, and Russia, with close attention paid to interpretations of events and the arguments the story raised in opinion journalism – in editorials, columns, letters to the editor, etc. We emphasise national mainstream outlets because the question of political legitimacy tends to be evaluated against national settings, even while the topic of surveillance is transnational.

In Chapter 2 we outline the theoretical and methodological framework of the study. Chapter 2 also briefly reports key findings from the six countries and identifies key threads in the transnational discourse. Generally speaking, in the dominant, mainstream media outlets, the NSA disclosures often prompted public discourse that defended existing practices and institutions. These reactions were frequently critical and suspicious of Snowden. Many media commentators concluded that systematic evidence of digital surveillance should not have been revealed. Supportive arguments for the leaks and institutional and policy reforms were more prominent in national media environments that enjoy a diversity of news outlets and well developed networks of civic activism. We also clearly noted that the explicit global outlook and readership policy of some news organisations (e.g. the *Guardian* and *Le Monde*) contributed to more critical debate. News environments that include networks of civic activists and communities of technology developers were also more likely to include criticism of surveillance practices. Where such networks have weaker presence and reach – as in Russia – the debate seemed decidedly less robust and consequential.

Beginning with Chapter 3, authors elaborate on the discussion by focusing on particular aspects of the debate as it was articulated in the countries where they live. Thus, instead of offering a sequence of strictly comparative country reports, this book aims to provide contextually anchored analyses on how discussions on security, privacy, and legitimacy highlight specific developments for journalism. To begin with, Katy Jones and Karin Wahl-Jorgensen look into the polarised public discussion the revelations caused in the UK. They show how relations between journalism and the state became a significant part of the story, and how questions about the autonomy of news organisations divided the journalistic field. In Chapter 4, Adrienne Russell and Silvio Waisbord analyse the dynamics of the US debate by focusing on symbolic exchanges between established media institutions and commentary coming from a broader swath of the digital and alternative news landscape. In their analysis, situated in the advanced hybrid media environment in the US, the authors introduce the explanatory concept of *news flashpoints*.

Chapters 5 and 6 present readings of the Snowden–NSA case in Continental Europe. Olivier Baisnée and Frédéric Nicolas pay particular attention to the intimate interplay between public opinion and the politics of surveillance. They analyse the dynamics of French public discourse against the aftermath of two terrorist attacks in 2015. They argue that this connection effectively downplayed debates on privacy and paved the way to a straightforward politics of securitisation. In Chapter 6, Johanna Möller and Anne Mollen look at Germany through the lens of public discourse on the politics of technology. Their analysis suggests that, while focus on national and international politics was vibrant, key political challenges related to digital technology were downplayed.

Chapters 7 and 8 explore contexts of state-controlled mainstream media where the NSA revelations were forcefully framed as issues of international controversy and national sovereignty. In Chapter 7, Haiyan Wang and Ruolin Fang analyse how interpretations in China of the Snowden–NSA event were mobilised to endorse Chinese public diplomacy. While highlighting the control mechanisms applied in the debate, their analysis suggests that a rhetoric linked to reputation becomes a viable and complex currency in contestations of international relations. Internet governance (Mueller, 2002; Balleste, 2015) is the central theme of Chapter 8, where Dmitry Yagodin analyses how alternative policies developed to challenge US domination of the internet emerged before Snowden's revelations and how such an initiative was fostered and exploited in Russian public debate.

These nationally anchored but transnationally relevant thematic analyses are not meant to provide exhaustive elaborations of domestic debates. They point to local conditions that made it possible for particular kinds of articulations to rise, but at the same time they suggest a list of key themes at play elsewhere. For instance, contesting the role of journalists politically and through arguments about national security was not unique to the UK. Understanding the networks of internationally operating newsrooms suggests ideologically similar fields of journalism across the sample. Hard-line arguments about security in France after the terror attacks have some similarity with those in UK.

Before venturing into the narrative of themes sketched above, we will use the rest of this introductory chapter to expand on key themes and concepts from media and journalism scholarship that inform our work. Below, we look at the leaks as an example of a global media event, an illustration of the emerging global culture of transparency, and as a moment that opens up crucial contestations about journalism. These themes help tease out the limits and possibilities of journalism's discursive power and situate the events and debates in historical context.

A particular kind of global media event

The Snowden–NSA affair seems intuitively to provide a notable example of a global media event where twists and turns unfold more *in* the media than anywhere else. Initially, Dayan and Katz (1992) developed the notion of media events to emphasise the role played by media in creating exceptional moments of concentrated public attention. They were particularly interested in ritualistic moments where the attention of large populations came together through media. For Dayan and Katz, the key focus was on all-nation encompassing moments in which the mass media were regarded as instrumental in connecting large populations to the imagined centre of society (cf. Couldry, 2003). In their initial theory, media events were pre-planned and their effects were amplified through the electronic mass media, radio, and television.

A quarter of a century later, the notion that media events rely on a distinction between spectacle and spectators and the emphasis on media event as mass mediated public ritual are still useful. Indeed, the media still enchant us with variations of 'conquests, competitions and coronations', as Dayan and Katz named the main genres. At the same time, in the contemporary networked media era the dynamics of media events have become more complicated. Attention-grasping events cannot be easily managed or orchestrated by individual producers. The audience is constantly courted to become part of the event through commenting, linking, sharing or other thus-far-unnamed practices (Couldry, 2012; Jenkins et al., 2010). Indeed, through new modes of communication and a wider range of communicative registers, the engaged audience can sometimes become a driving force of the event (cf. Papacharissi, 2015).

Media events, then, have become more volatile and potentially more disruptive of the social order. They are no longer simply moments of restoration and celebration of social order but sometimes momentary breakdowns of that order. As media events tied to terror attacks clearly show, the logic and dynamics of the media event can become a part of a moment of disruption.

The Snowden–NSA event illustrates these new conditions in several ways. It clearly escapes the initial national and ritualistic frameworks of traditional media events. The focus of attention it creates is global from the outset. Also, the questions it poses are transnational, as is the 'public' the event concerns; that is, the people *affected* by the US security surveillance and future surveillance (cf. Fraser, 2014). The story of digital snooping is instrumental in articulating suspicion of the government not merely nationally but also internationally. The Snowden story does something more complicated than mainly reinforcing unifying national identities. The tension between the national and the transnational cuts through this book, suggesting that global media events need to be studied as moments where publics are introduced into arenas and into debates that are simultaneously national and transnational.

Although the flow of Snowden-related scoops was driven by a group of skilful and openly passionate journalists, it would be hard to claim that the event was orchestrated in advance. Rather, it was propelled by a sometimes odd combination of occurrences with trajectories of their own. These included, for instance, extraordinary episodes (the detainment of Glenn Greenwald's partner David Miranda at Heathrow Airport, MI5 destroying the hard drive disks at the *Guardian's* editorial office), unexpected contradictions (pitting close political allies in the US and Germany against each other), and uneasy alliances (Snowden's asylum in Putin's Russia). As discussed throughout this book, an event became many events, depending on the context of interpretation.

The NSA event is a particular kind of media event because it so deeply involves the media *as* media. As we point out above, it is a controversy about privacy, and therefore about conceptions of the public, which are key to providing journalism with its professional legitimacy. In covering Snowden and the NSA, the media build an event and a drama – inside which it also performs itself, providing self-commentary and meta-coverage on the role of journalism. It is also a story in which the field of journalism (cf. Benson and Neveu, 2005; Bourdieu, 1993) is contested and divided as people disagree over what news media ought and ought not to do.

Contestations of journalism

Snowden drew lessons from his immediate predecessors in the emerging digital-era culture of whistle-blowers and leakers, and his actions intensified already aggressive government reactions to the phenomenon (cf. Downie, 2013). Unlike Julian Assange from WikiLeaks, Snowden consciously chose to sustain the distinction between journalists and whistle-blowers. He also chose to align with journalists and news organisations that could not only reach a large audience but also could act as more complicated targets for immediate counter-measures.

> So the idea I thought about here was that we need institutions working beyond borders in multiple jurisdictions simply to complicate legally to the point that the journalists could play games, legally and journalistically more effectively and more quickly than the government could play legalistic claims to interfere with them. (Snowden in Bell, 2016)

This strategy points directly to a key line of contestation that the case placed under the spotlight. The revelations exposed different ways in which media negotiate their relationship to the state. While most news organisations in the West claim to be critical and autonomous of politicians, their relationship to issues of national security – and thus their relationship to the *security state* rather than the *political state* – proved to be more complicated. The most dramatic stand-offs, in this respect, took place between the *Guardian* and the Government Communications Headquarters (GCHQ), which commanded the symbolic destruction of hard drives at the newspaper's headquarters. British intelligence also arrested and interrogated Glenn Greenwald's partner, David Miranda, at Heathrow Airport, confiscating and searching his computer. Many media outlets in the UK and the US chose to defend the claim made by security officials that the leaks and the journalists working on them had acted irresponsibly (see Chapters 3 and 4). These episodes demonstrate how the state–journalism relationship divided the field of journalism *internally*. As the privacy–security debate continues, this line is constantly renegotiated.

Given that the Snowden–NSA case set the focus on national security as a topic of journalism, it also created clear differences *between* media outlets in national fields of journalism. Often it moved right-leaning papers to emphasise views of the security community and provide less space altogether for the coverage. In some cases, it also showed lines of demarcation inside newsrooms, between editors and reporters, such as in the case of the *Washington Post*. Even as the newspaper published key NSA revelations, an editorial signed by the 'editorial board' (1 July 2013) called for 'stopping damaging revelations or the dissemination of intelligence to adversaries'. It also suggested that Snowden was 'a naïve hacker' and should give himself up to US authorities.[6] While such views can, of course, be well grounded, for Greenwald and Snowden this suggested the close proximity of mainstream editors to the established institutions and structures of power, and thus it marked a violation of the professional autonomy of journalism. In an interview three years after the leaks, Snowden expressed his highly critical view of the mainstream press:

> *anybody who's worked in the news industry, either directly or even peripherally, has seen journalists – or, more directly, editors – who are terrified, who hold back a story, who don't want to publish a detail, who want to wait for the lawyers, who are concerned with liability.* (Snowden in Bell, 2016)

Snowden's words resonate with another distinction surfaced in the debate, one concerning varying ideals about reporting and articulated in an exchange between Greenwald and Bill Keller, former editor-in-chief of the *New York Times*. The exchange was preceded by the announcement in October 2013 that Greenwald would leave the *Guardian* and, together with Laura Poitras and Jeremy Scahill (and through financial support from the eBay founder Pierre Omidyar), found a new outlet, the *Intercept*. This prompted Keller to ask if the new platform would be a 'partisan endeavour'. In a much-circulated exchange, Keller claimed that Greenwald's background, first as a lawyer, then as a blogger and columnist, influenced his approach to reporting. He said 'Greenwald's writing proceeds from a clearly stated point of view',[7] and thus departs from journalism, which puts 'a premium on aggressive but impartial reporting' and leaves opinions to opinion pages. Greenwald (2014: 231) viewed the distinction as a fallacy. For him, the relevant demarcation line resides between 'journalists who candidly reveal their opinions and those who conceal them, pretending they have none'.[8]

This juxtaposition – neutral reporting and opinionated investigations – reflects a classic distinction in journalism history and attempts to problematise it. In the first line of criticism, it has been argued that 'neutrality' is not much more than a style of journalistic expression in which the journalist distances himself or herself from a subject, and this effectively sustains dominant ideologies and the status quo in society. A more contemporary criticism lines up with contemporary observations that a viable, powerful challenge to the dominant mainstream journalism model could be emerging in the form of more aggressively assertive opinionated journalism (cf. Nerone 2015b). Indeed, Jay Rosen (2013), who took part in the work to build up the *Intercept*, argues that Greenwald embodies a developing model of journalism that fits better with the way communication, attention, and audience participation is organised in the web environment. In the digital age, the key to the profession for Greenwald or Snowden, as well as for many journalists, lies in demonstrating expertise and establishing a 'personal franchise' and the ability to create a following.

Global investigative journalism

The varied and often clashing reception that greeted the NSA scoops underlined long-building divisions and tensions in the field of journalism. Reporters working the story were criticised as activists and even traitors in some quarters, but they were also awarded Pulitzer Prizes. The tensions tied to the reception of reporting within the field raises a question about whether the Snowden–NSA reporting might be different from earlier forms of investigative journalism to a significant degree.

The history of investigative journalism stretches at least as far back as the twentieth-century idea of journalism as a profession (Waisbord, 2013). The muckrakers of the early 1900s in the US were a product of the progressive belief in the power of information and independent journalism. Investigative journalism rose to its zenith in the 1970s during the 'high modernism' period (Hallin, 1992). In the West, investigation became a lofty bearer of the demanding values of journalism and it balanced journalists' structural dependency on bureaucracies as their primary sources. Watergate, the story that led to the impeachment of the world's then most powerful politician, President Richard Nixon, marked the mythical and celebrated high point.

The Snowden–NSA affair captures a critical moment against this history. First, investigative journalism – capable, committed, and backed by sufficient resources to follow vague leaks and peruse piles of documents – seems to be passing, at least at many legacy news organisations. Due to new economic and technological realities, fewer newsrooms can afford to allocate their resources to assignments that cost more money than they generate in revenue and reputation in return. In the fast-paced digital environment, economic and symbolic rewards brought by investigative scoops seem smaller and more short-lived than before. As a response, some investigative journalists have reportedly left large newsrooms to try and seize opportunities in the niche news market operated by start-up companies or flexible cooperative projects (Anderson et al., 2013). Greenwald's migration from the *Guardian* to the *Intercept* is a potential example.

Concern about the withering mainstream resources of investigative journalism and the moral limits of its professional critique shed light on the Snowden story, particularly as it relates to investigative journalism. The Greenwald–Poitras partnership, in this respect, is very different from that of Woodward–Bernstein. Greenwald and Poitras were selected by Snowden due to their previous political advocacy relating to government surveillance policies. They had already developed a public moral stance on the issue as part of their 'brand', and their reputation as investigative journalists was built mostly at a distance from traditional mainstream media. Yet Greenwald and Poitras were both connected to major news organisations: Greenwald to the *Guardian* and Poitras to the *Washington Post* and *Der Spiegel*.

This professional alliance proved organisationally effective and strategically useful; it helped pool resources and decentralise the analytical work to people working in different time zones and political contexts. This enabled them to produce continuous rounds of news stories, and the network structure helped fend off institutional and legal pressures from national governments. Despite the mutual benefits, this alliance also created internal tensions, as Greenwald's (2014) version of the story clearly describes. Given their suspicions towards their allies at mainstream outlets, Greenwald and Poitras finally chose to break away and start the *Intercept*.

The cooperation seems to represent an evolutionary phase in the recent globalisation of journalistic investigations, as it directly or indirectly paved the way for the release in 2016 of the Panama Papers. In that case, an enormous trove of documents from the law firm Mossack Fonseca revealed a web of offshore shell companies designed for clients, mostly members of the global elite, seeking in many cases to evade taxes and hoard wealth. The evidence for the disclosure was obtained from an anonymous source by the German newspaper *Süddeutsche Zeitung*, which shared the documents with the International Consortium of Investigative Journalists (ICIJ). The ICIJ then distributed the materials to a large network of international partners. More than 370 journalists in more than 100 news outlets from eighty countries used encryption technology to work on the leaks for months without exposing their source.

A general rationale of investigative journalism suggests that disclosures fuel public moral outrage, prompting legitimate controversy and calls for reform. In the case of the Panama Papers, the outrage emanated from the fact that global businesses make use of exclusive practices that enable companies and individual investors to profit at the taxpayer's expense. This observation in turn would trigger public debate on opposing practices designed expressly for the purpose of dodging taxes. In the Snowden affair, however, the lines tying the story to moral outrage and action appear more ambiguous. For those who are concerned with civil liberties, the massive surveillance constitutes a breach of the public trust. From the viewpoint of those who designed the surveillance systems, however, there was no breach because the system protected the citizens. By drawing from transnational interpretations concerning the key values of journalism – publicity, accountability and solidarity (Ettema and Glasser, 1998) – globally positioned investigative journalists highlighted such contradictions.

In the aftermath of the Snowden revelations, the US authorities' responses ranged from blunt and offended to sophisticatedly nuanced. An example of the former was provided by Director of National Intelligence James R. Clapper:

> Many of the recent articles based on leaked classified documents have painted an inaccurate and misleading picture of the Intelligence Community. The reality is that the men and women at the National Security Agency and across the Intelligence Community are abiding by the law, respecting the rights of citizens and doing everything they can to help keep our nation safe. (Clapper [2013] quoted in Fidler, 2015: 173–4)

President Barack Obama's *Remarks on Review of Signals Intelligence*, from January 2014, introduced a more cautiously weaved narrative to the post-9/11 world, and the need for more public oversight of surveillance capacities. First, he pointed to the inherent role of secrecy in intelligence work.

> Intelligence agencies cannot function without secrecy, which makes their work less subject to public debate. … In the absence of institutional

requirements for regular debate and oversight … the danger of government overreach becomes more acute. (Obama [2014] quoted in Fidler, 2015: 321)

He then went on to bring in a more human and moral element to surveillance.

[T]he men and women at the NSA know that if another 9/11 or a massive cyber-attack occurs, they will be asked, by the Congress and the media, why they failed to connect the dots. What sustains those who work at NSA and our other intelligence agencies through all these pressures is the knowledge that their professionalism and dedication play a central role in the defence of our nation. … Our nation's defence depends in part on the fidelity of those entrusted with our nation's secrets. If any individual who objects to government policy can take it into their own hands to publicly disclose classified information, then we will not be able to keep our people safe, or conduct foreign policy. (Ibid. 321–2)

In regard to security, the state suggests that to some extent values such as privacy, individual freedom, and claims for transparency and accountability are a form of historical luxury. Ultimately, these values depend on the security function of the state. When the primary virtue is at peril, secondary virtues must stand back. This raises the question of whether transparency and public oversight can coexist with surveillance without undermining its utility. As a result, the category of national interest – and security as its core element – remains a powerful vehicle in controlling public discourse and disciplining (investigative) journalism. In the Snowden–NSA case, national interest sometimes translated as immediate legal pressure to break source protections and use diplomatic interventions to sanction and isolate individuals such as Snowden or Julian Assange. On a rhetorical level, this threat was also eminent when Rusbridger, editor of the *Guardian,* faced an official inquiry and was asked: 'Do you love this country?' (See *Guardian,* 3 December 2013).[9]

Event or transformation?

The most common criticism about me today – that I am too naïve, that I have too much faith in government, that I have too much faith in the press. I don't see that as a weakness. I am naïve, but I think that idealism is critical to achieving change, ultimately not of policy, but of culture, right? Because we can change this or that law, we can change this or that policy or program, but at the end of the day, it's the values of the people in these institutions that are producing these programs. (Snowden in Bell, 2016)

In a radical reading, the moral outrage and vibrant public discourse raised by the NSA revelations suggest a possible newly found political energy and even the emergence of a 'global public'. In this spirit, recent disclosures instigated by leaks, the Snowden case among them, may be seen as part of the counter-struggle for new articulations of the boundaries between the private and public realms. In this sense, the NSA exposures are a good candidate for a *historical event*, a moment that can launch 'already dislocated' structures (institutions, actors, meanings) towards new articulations (see Sewell, 2005).

By bringing momentarily into the spotlight some of the contradictions between beliefs and practices and by forcing institutions and actors to justify their positions, the revelations have prompted important questions. A radical reading of the potential of the event would suggest that, in the decades to come, the NSA revelations will be referred to as an important milestone, that it encouraged relatively widespread development of personal encryption skills, politicised the role of large internet companies, sensitised consumers to their rights and led to incremental but important policy reforms in surveillance oversight. In addition, such a reading would see the NSA case enhance critical and self-reflective discussion about journalism, nationally and transnationally.

A more cautious reading of the event would perceive the evidence of change as less convincing. While there has certainly been a lot of debate, there are few clear signs of structural change. In the global power struggle, authoritarian governments have been able to discredit internet freedom and argue for more national and paternalistic control (see Chapters 7 and 8). Reforms of surveillance practices have not been dramatic, and in some contexts – for apparently different reasons but in a parallel way – surveillance powers have actually been enhanced (France and Russia, see Chapters 5 and 8). The process Snowden's revelations set in motion has, at best, been a volatile one, including for those involved in the exposé. Snowden's own immunity to legal and extra-legal pressures remains doubtful. The legal ground on which the newspapers cooperating with Snowden have mounted what would seem traditional defences seems less solid than in times past – and ready to shift from day to day.

Against Snowden's optimistic opinion about the arrival of a productive cultural change, there are much more sober or pessimistic diagnoses. Many policy and law analysts, particularly in the US, argue that governmental activities like diplomacy, military action and intelligence operations are never conducted transparently and that the courts and Congress, the entities responsible for formal intelligence oversight, are unlikely to effectively perform those functions (Sagar, 2013).

Our strategy in this book is to take seriously the *possibility* that tensions dramatised in the NSA case are part of an ongoing structural renegotiation of the distinction between public and private spaces. This means that the case offers an entry point to the tensions and contradictions at the core of our political imagination and its discursive structures. The case is focused on security in an era that is predominantly cast as one of terror and the war on terror and where the notion of 'hybrid' war redefines resources and risks of security. This arguably takes the case to the core terrain of power and raises the stakes. The questions at play – institutional, material, and symbolic structures – have to do with a potential historical transformation. Even if we do not know where future developments will take us, the rearticulations of the private–public distinction can turn out to be transformative. In retrospect, we might come, theoretically but justifiably, to compare them to earlier transformations: the oft-romanticised emergence of the bourgeois public sphere or the consequent rearticulation of that idealised conversational public into the quantified and atomised notion of 'public opinion' in the poll democracies of the twentieth century. In this sense, the NSA revelations may come to be understood as a historical, singular, contingent but still 'historical' episode that contributed to consequences beyond its immediate context (cf. Sewell, 2005: 227–8).

In order to elaborate the dynamic between specific events and structural forces and the different pace of consequences events can engender, it is worthwhile to look for a moment at the role of large internet service providers in the controversy. As *The Economist* neatly put it in the midst of the Snowden revelations, 'Surveillance is Advertising's New Business Model' (13 September 2014),[10] pointing out that the monetising logic of internet services relies on individual targeting and that the interests of internet service providers and tools available to them do not differ from those of intelligence agencies. There is no necessary reason that this should lead to a dramatic conflict between corporate and state actors but, in the aftermath of the intensified security and privacy debate, it has. As giant internet service providers have branded themselves (and their audiences' trust) with ideas of individuality, creativity, and freedom, the NSA revelations about their data being harvested by the security apparatus presented potentially damaging revelations.

Business concerns prompted an open letter from US-based technology companies to President Obama in December 2013. It declared that the companies were preparing to deploy the latest encryption technology 'to prevent unauthorised surveillance of our networks and pushing back government requests to ensure that they are legal and reasonable in scope' (quoted in Fidler, 2015: 150).

Tension between the security community and internet companies has a long genealogy. Ideas of counter-culture, creativity, and innovative entrepreneurship were forged prior to the internet (cf. Turner, 2006). As the breakthrough of the World Wide Web coincided with a temporary pause in the Cold War, 'technologies of freedom' became the core metaphor for describing the digitising world. Through popular technology writing and macro-sociological accounts, the image of the simultaneously destructive and liberating power of digitisation has become an essential part of our social imagination. It has developed into a dominant mega-trend that seems to have a life of its own, reshaping thinking about economics and citizenship (e.g. Benkler, 2006; Papacharissi, 2010). As we have enthusiastically fastened our lives to the web, the faith that more freedom and prosperity will be delivered through digitisation has grown exponentially.

By dramatically pointing to the potential of digital communication technologies for surveillance and control, Snowden's revelations demonstrated for a much larger public that there is another side to open, interactive, personally gratifying internet usage, wherein users are secretly monitored by state and corporate actors. Snowden's main objective was to underline the link between digitised spheres of the market and the state. It is one thing to feel the flattering or disturbing effects of being addressed by advertisers in an overtly targeted manner. It is another thing to realise that this invasion of privacy is not only influencing your consumer choices but also gauging your loyalty to the state. This general awareness heats up debate about the 'trade-off' between privacy and security, and about how best to address concerns (Solove, 2011).

Tensions between internet companies and governments are real. The spring 2016 stand-off between Apple and the FBI on whether or not and how to access a terrorist shooter's encrypted iPhone saw these two powerful forces butt heads publicly about what course of action best served the public interest. The Snowden–NSA case brought into sharper focus the ties that stretched between the government and technology giants and the way the two sides negotiated a back and forth balance of power. In June 2015, Ben Wizner, Snowden's legal adviser and Director of the American Civil Liberties Union's (ACLU) Speech, Privacy and Technology Project, argued that this tension might be an element in a new system of surveillance oversight. He also recognised the complexity of the role played by technology giants.

> There are some people in the anti-surveillance movement ... who think essentially that we have picked the wrong target. [That] the bigger threat to free society, in the long term, will come from the corporations. ... The real hope for us is if those entities take on each other. We really will need the government's help to protect us as consumers. Only the government can really ensure that we will have fairness in due process in confronting the effects of big data which you already see. ... At the same time, there will be no legislative surveillance reform without Google and Facebook and Apple and those companies being in our coalition. Civil society doesn't have the power to get that change through legislatively without having them as allies. There's a strategic necessity in separating those battles rather than having them together. (Wizner, 2015b)

The controversy between the tech industry and government(s) is just one example of several structural tensions that shape the discussion about privacy and security and the consequent rearticulation of the journalism environment. This book analyses the Snowden–NSA affair as part of a larger exploration of public debate around privacy and security. Our overarching aim is not to explain what happened, nor to argue for any particular formula balancing freedom, security, privacy, and surveillance. Rather, the book aims to leverage study of the Snowden–NSA revelations as media event to advance thinking about global communication, media technologies, and democracy.

Notes

1 See Glenn Greenwald and Laura Poitras, 'Edward Snowden: "The US government will say I aided our enemies" – video interview'. *Guardian*,

8 June 2016. http://www.theguardian.com/world/video/2013/jul/08/edward-snowden-video-interview. 'NSA whistleblower Edward Snowden: "I don't want to live in a society that does these sort of things" – video.' *Guardian*, 9 June 2013. http://www.theguardian.com/world/video/2013/jun/09/nsa-whistleblower-edward-snowden-interview-video. Paul Lewis and Karen McVeigh, 'Edward Snowden: what we know about the source behind the NSA files leak.' *Guardian*, 9 June 2016. http://www.theguardian.com/world/2013/jun/11/edward-snowden-what-we-know-nsa (accessed May 2016).

2 There are several versions of timelines highlighting the key episodes in this narrative (Gurnow, 2014: 285–91; Chadwick and Collister, 2014).

3 http://enhancinglife.uchicago.edu/blog/reassessing-the-price-of-connection See also Couldry and Hepp, 2017.

4 On 7 May 2016, a US Federal Appeals court ruled the NSA program that systematically collects phone records in bulk, revealed by Snowden, is illegal under the Patriot Act. *New York Times*, 7 May 2014. http://www.nytimes.com/2015/05/08/us/nsa-phone-records-collection-ruled-illegal-by-appeals-court.html?_r=0.

5 '"This Award is for Snowden": Greenwald, Poitras Accept Polk Honor for Exposing NSA Surveillance.' Democracy Now. http://www.democracynow.org/2014/4/14/this_award_is_for_snowden_glenn (accessed May 2016).

6 Roy Greenslade, 'Edward Snowden's leaks cause editorial split at the Washington Post.' *Guardian*, 5 July 2016. http://www.theguardian.com/media/greenslade/2013/jul/05/edward-snowden-washington-post. David Sirota, 'Meet the "Journalists Against Journalism" Club!' Salon, 2 July 2013. http://www.salon.com/2013/07/02/meet_the_journalists_against_journalism_club (accessed Dec. 2015).

7 See Greg Mitchell, 29 Oct. 2013, *The Nation*. http://www.thenation.com/article/glenn-greenwald-vs-bill-keller-future-journalism. Bill Keller, 'Is Glenn Greenwald the future of news?' *New York Times*, 28 Oct. 2013. http://www.nytimes.com/2013/10/28/opinion/a-conversation-in-lieu-of-a-column.html?smid=tw-shareand_r=1and (accessed 22 Jan. 2016).

8 Later, Snowden (in Bell, 2016), in fact takes the distinction even further, drawing a line between 'reporters' and 'journalists'.

9 Alan Rusbridger, 'MPs' questions to Alan Rusbridger: do you love this country?' *Guardian*, 3 Dec. 2013. http://www.theguardian.com/media/2013/dec/03/keith-vaz-alan-rusbridger-love-country-nsa (accessed Aug. 2016).

10 http://www.economist.com/news/leaders/21616953-surveillance-advertising-industrys-new-business-model-privacy-needs-better (accessed May 2016).

2

Two Dimensions of Global Discourse: Domestication and Justification

Risto Kunelius, Heikki Heikkilä, and Adrienne Russell
with Karin Wahl-Jorgensen, Katy Jones, Anne Mollen,
Johanna Möller, Frédéric Nicolas, Olivier Baisnée, Haiyan
Wang, Dennis Leung, Ruolin Fang, and Dmitry Yagodin

The NSA revelations sparked a global media event focused on national security where journalism was one of the key actors. It is the kind of story that underlines the way journalism is woven into the complicated dynamics of the public sphere, where the assumed intentions of news organisations and their impact on policies are heavily scrutinised.

While the Snowden–NSA case has proved to be extraordinary in many ways, concerns about political legitimacy are everyday concerns in the media. One useful analytical model for thinking about political legitimacy in the context of journalism is Daniel Hallin's (1986) study on the coverage of Vietnam War in the US at the end of 1960s. In it, Hallin outlined a model of three discursive spheres where public discussion operates. At the centre of the model (see Figure 2.1) lies the sphere of *consensus*, which contains truths, values, and facts that are considered uncontroversial and unchallenged in a given society. Here reside views that do not need to be publicly defended – such as the evil of terrorism or the primary importance of national security. Consensual views are culturally contextual, and the scope of this sphere tends to vary from one topic to another. At the outskirts of the model lies the sphere of *illegitimacy*. Here reside issues, arguments, and actors that are deemed idiosyncratic, eccentric, or outright dangerous and therefore not worthy of defence. One of the roles of mainstream journalism is to negotiate this border, keeping deviant themes and actors out of the media or by describing them as unacceptable, radical, or just plain irrational. Between these zones lies the

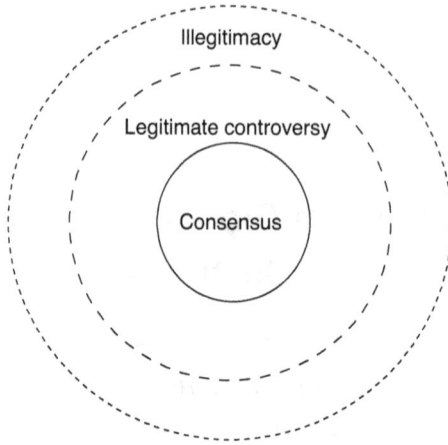

Figure 2.1 Spheres of public debate (Hallin)

essential part of the public sphere, the terrain of *legitimate controversy*, a sphere constructed of topics, actors, and viewpoints where disagreement is acceptable. The sphere of legitimate controversy results from ongoing selection and exclusion of themes and social actors.

The dominant understanding of how issues and viewpoints are situated in the realms of controversy, consensus, and illegitimacy depends on power relations within a given society. The media serve as sites in which policies and implicit rules of public debate can be challenged. Therefore, legitimacy – denoting public consent to the political system and the output of policies – is both a condition and product of public debate. This model remains applicable to the contemporary media environment. However, given the intensely transnational nature of the debate on digital surveillance raised by the Snowden–NSA revelations, the model could be usefully updated to treat the tensions between national and transnational forces shaping global media events. The complementary notions of domestication and transnationalisation point to different aspects in contemporary journalism and media events.

There exists, as yet, no space nor platform where we could expect to find genuinely 'global' debate. Instead, we overwhelmingly engage in national debates strongly shaped by culturally and politically distinct traditions and circumstances – and national perspectives tend to play a particularly powerful role in shaping debates on security. *Domestication* denotes a set of practices with which journalists translate foreign news about 'them' (the people of other nations) into news about 'us' (the people of your own nation) (Nossek, 2004, see below).

Without acute awareness of the forces of domestication, it is difficult to fully grasp the dynamics of global news events. It is, however, not sufficient to look merely at who and which viewpoints were presented in the national public spheres. It is also important to explore any characteristics shared across national debates. In the analysis below, then, we try also to locate some principles of *justification* (see Boltanski and Thévenot, 2006), which point to abstract cultural resources of argumentation not necessarily bound by national power relations, to find features that go beyond domestication.

The empirical data and analytical framework

In order to understand the NSA revelations as global news event and as a combination of national public debates, we look at the debate as it unfolded in six national contexts: the United States, United Kingdom, France, Germany, Russia, and China/Hong Kong. These countries played key roles in the story, even as they viewed the revelations of the story through often very different political lenses. This study is not an exploration of news reporting that would centre on which social and political actors enjoy access to news, or how their views are covered (cf. Ericson et al., 1989). This is, instead, research focusing on media *debate*.

For the empirical analysis, we collected opinion pieces published by national outlets on the early stages of the revelations, from June 2013 to February 2014. In the initial stage, all coverage related to the topic was gathered, after which the analytical focus was set on specific peak moments of the given national debate. In the last phase, the volume of national samples was narrowed to 80–100 items in each country.

Given their distinct national characteristics, the search for mainstream opinions varied from one country to another. In the UK, for instance, the analysis focused on national newspapers only and tried to capture the diversity and assumed polarisation between the elite and popular press. The analysis covers seven newspapers: the *Guardian,* the *Independent,* the *Daily Telegraph, The Times,* the *Daily Mail,* the *Daily Mirror,* and the *Sun.* In the US, the empirical focus was on two newspapers of record, the *New York Times* and the *Wall Street Journal,* and then broadened by a selection of outlets of distinct voice, namely, *Mother Jones* (a left-of-centre news magazine), *National Review* (a right-of-centre news magazine), Electronic

Frontier Foundation (a non-profit online civil liberties advocacy group), and the Verge (a tech-focused news outlet).

In France and Germany, the analysis in this chapter is limited to elite newspapers: *Le Monde*, *Le Figaro*, and *Libération* in France, and *Frankfurter Allgemeine Zeitung* and *Süddeutsche Zeitung* in Germany. The analysis materials for Russia include two state-controlled outlets: the governmental daily newspaper *Rossiyskaya Gazeta* and the most watched national television channel (Channel One), and two more independent outlets: the popular newspaper *Moskovskij Komsomolets* and the largest online newspaper *Lenta*. The analysis on the case in China captures three variations of official voices: the elite official voice (*People's Daily*), the official voice in popular form (*Global Times*), and the official voice directed towards an international audience and published in English (*China Daily* and *Global Times*). In Hong Kong, three Chinese-language newspapers, *Apple Daily*, *Ming Pao* and *Wen Wei Po*, and one English newspaper, *South China Morning Post* (SCMP), were studied. The Chinese papers represent liberal, moderate and conservative voices, respectively, whereas SCMP played a more special role. It was the only local newspaper to conduct an exclusive, widely cited, interview with Snowden during his stay in Hong Kong.

Each piece in the core sample was studied with an eye towards five empirical questions. The first one aimed to capture the contextual background of the argument. Two following questions aimed at detecting the relevance of the argument for the national public debate from the perspective of domestication: what was the problem addressed in the text, and how and by whom could it be solved? Two remaining questions try to get hold of the broader socio-political principles that justify the argumentation of a given author. Although articulated as part of national contexts and debates, these principles also potentially point to more transnational value vocabularies in place of the sphere of legitimate controversy (see Table 2.1).

Table 2.1 Research questions for the empirical analysis

1. What is the contextual background for the argument?	
Domestication patterns	**Transnational justifications**
2. What is the problem addressed?	4. What conceptual distinctions is the argument based on?
3. What are the solutions proposed?	5. What are the principles that help justify the conclusions?

Below, we describe the general findings of the analysis, reading them first against the notion of domestication, and then in relation to principles of justification.

The pull of domestication: six versions of the NSA

Since Galtung and Ruge-Holmboe's (1965) seminal study on the way news values shape international coverage, the dominant view has been that media tend to represent globally significant events against their proximity and relevance to national politics or economy. This pattern of professional judgement does not merely refer to *what* is regarded as newsworthy. It also applies to *how* events are interpreted and given meaning. In journalism research and media studies, these broader patterns of sense-making are often discussed as *domestication*. Originally borrowed from zoology, the notion refers to how events happening afar need to be culturally tamed before they can be meaningfully understood back home. This practice is reportedly at the centre of the generic contract between producers and consumers of news, as Gurevitch et al. (1991) noted: 'In order to be judged newsworthy, an event must be anchored in a narrative framework that is already familiar to and recognisable by newsmen [sic] as well as by audiences' (quoted in Clausen, 2003: 15).

Domestication draws support from journalism's function of informing the public, not merely about issues close to the members of the audience but also those for which they may have limited knowledge. In doing so, domestication also fills the gap between foreign and domestic by creating cues for politicisation that are taken up by local political parties, civic organisations, experts, citizens, and so on. Thus, domestication is – or at least aims to be – functional to democracy as it facilitates and contributes to political debate. At the same time, domestication may also confine debate, as it 'tends to compress it to fit into the range of debate between decisive institutional power blocks' (Bennett, 1990: 106). In an ironic twist on the democratic ideal, Bennett writes:

> *Modern public opinion can be thought of as an 'index' constructed from the distribution of dominant institutional voices as recorded in the mass media. By adopting such an opinion index, the media have helped create a political world that is, culturally speaking, upside-down. It is a world in which governments are able to define their own publics and*

where 'democracy' becomes whatever the government ends up doing.
(1990: 124–5)

The coverage from the six countries on which we focused is distinct in each case, but there were also some affinities. In the US and the UK, the leaks were politicised intensively, setting up tension between the journalism and the intelligence communities, and inside the field of journalism as well. This was partly because both national governments played a key part in the exposed surveillance networks. In France and Germany, the national discussions took off from a different position, where the initial culprits were not national politicians. The first reactions articulated outrage over the reach of US-initiated surveillance. Given that China and Russia share a position of power in opposition to the US, in these countries the NSA case prompted strong defence of national sovereignty and explicit criticism of Western powers.

The United States

In the US, the case naturally triggered a great deal of coverage, not least because of national relevance: Snowden is an American citizen and was a contract employee of the US agency running the surveillance programme at the heart of the story. The case shed critical light on US foreign and security policies, raising questions about the legitimacy of those policies and about their implications for international relations.

In the opinion sections of newspapers, magazines, and online outlets, the incident brought up old and new questions about democratic rights as well as the rights and obligations of the government and the private sector in the post-9/11 world. Interpretations of events and views on the topics of surveillance, national security, transparency, and privacy clashed and competed. The coverage raised a series of questions that escaped straightforward and empirically convincing answers. Did secret surveillance by the NSA produce information that prevented terrorist attacks? How transparent should the intelligence programmes be? Can information seen as tied to national security be obtained without violating the rights of American citizens? Who owns information and/or decides the limits between the private and the public interest? What is the correct interpretation of the First Amendment on these matters? Should private companies comply with the government's plans to monitor citizen communication? And what role should a journalist and news outlet play in reporting on the story and advocating government transparency?

Predictably, answers to these questions and the treatment of the key themes that drove the debate varied outlet to outlet, according to editorial positions. At the onset of the story, the focus in the *New York Times* and *Wall Street Journal* was on the legality and constitutionality of the programme – specifically on whether NSA surveillance accorded with the text of the Patriot Act and the Fourth Amendment.[1] Questions also concerned the effectiveness of surveillance programmes in curtailing terrorist attacks, and whether the effectiveness of surveillance was its own justification. Opinions in the *New York Times* were largely critical of the NSA and Obama's cautious reaction to the revelations. In the *Wall Street Journal*, nearly every related opinion piece and column argued that US national security depends on government surveillance, and that Snowden put Americans in danger by betraying national secrets. Several pieces pointed to a legal precedent in which the US Supreme Court interpreted the Constitution in a way that allowed for mass surveillance.

By the end of 2013, however, both papers expanded the debate to include issues related to the need for checks and balances in response to new technology and to insure against abuses of power on the part of the government. In both papers, the debate was essentially represented as one between whether the courts or the politicians should have the power to decide what NSA activities are permissible. While the issue of privacy was frequently touched on in both papers, neither offered a clear definition of it or touched on the moral and ethical considerations associated with invasions of privacy. The elite newspapers followed traditional news forms and practices when reporting on the story – echoing the views of the domestic bureaucratic elite, limiting points of view to the opinion columns, and aiming to report the story as it unfolded.

National Review and *Mother Jones*, national magazines at opposite poles of the ideological spectrum, echoed the points of view and themes of the *Wall Street Journal* and the *New York Times*, respectively. The overtly opinionated style of the magazines, however, allowed for open critique of political leaders, media coverage, and the NSA programmes revealed by Snowden. They also introduced new themes and a wider range of perspectives to the surveillance debate. *National Review* repeatedly called for the prosecution of Snowden, criticised journalists for their role in facilitating the leaks, and argued for the constitutionality of the NSA's secret programme. *Mother Jones* provided a very different set of arguments about the broader significance of the revelations. In that view, leaks and whistle-blowing were defended as the most effective means of obtaining information about government activities, and pointing out that citizens want more transparency from their government.

Mother Jones also provided more nuanced analysis of the issues surrounding notions of privacy, surveillance, and government/citizen relations, moving beyond legal arguments and publishing corrections in response to official statements and media reports. Electronic Frontier Foundation (EFF) and the Verge offered some of the most detailed treatment of the technological and legal issues related to the story, and gave a platform for the most outspoken critics of media and political leaders. These outlets also put their focus on the role of the technology industry in digital surveillance and in attempts at its regulation.

Overall, in the US, *what* was covered was connected to official debates, while *how* it was covered was largely shaped by the editorial positions of the given news outlet. In this hybrid landscape, there was abundant meta-coverage: critiques and debates about the specific stories as well as about the roles and responsibilities of journalism, often pitting old and new journalism actors and styles against one another (for broader implications of the developments in the US, see Chapter 5).

The United Kingdom

The UK media played a unique role in Snowden–NSA case globally, due partly to the prominent role of journalist Glenn Greenwald and the *Guardian*, where he published his stories, but also partly because of the central role in the story played by the US–UK surveillance alliance. Given its key role in the process, the *Guardian* covered and commented on the events much more than other British newspapers. The media attention to the issue was clearly divided between the quality and popular press. The quality newspapers (the *Independent*, *The Times*, the *Daily Telegraph* and the *Guardian*) were most concerned with the initial leaks but monitored the later policy developments consistently. The popular press (the *Sun*, *Daily Mirror*, and *Daily Mail*), on the other hand, placed most of its focus on a particular incident in the case: the detention of Glenn Greenwald's partner, David Miranda, at Heathrow Airport in August 2013.

The discourse in the UK media was centred on the issue of oversight of the government and its security agencies. The debate, on the whole, was characterised by strong defence of surveillance. These legitimations, however, were based on a complex chain of argumentation linked to a call for greater transparency, oversight, and accountability of the state. Crucially, the discussion was laid on the premise that surveillance is acceptable, as long as the right checks and balances are in place, and citizens are adequately informed of intelligence activities.

Another dominant theme was the debate on civil rights; that is, the protection of citizen privacy and freedom of speech. These issues were discussed extensively in the left-leaning press. In this context, the threats of authoritarianism were projected onto the US rather than onto the UK. By contrast, newspapers on the right maintained for instance that the destruction of hard-drives at the *Guardian* was not a sign of domestic authoritarianism but that the MI5 had operated in the name of national security. Commentators warned the media against revealing state secrets since the practice is contrary to the national interest.

The security theme also appeared alongside arguments relating to press freedom and press censorship. This was particularly the case in connection to the detention of David Miranda in July 2013. Miranda's detention was justified by the UK government on the grounds that he was carrying material that 'could aid terrorism', constituting a threat to national security. Some authors argued that the documents Miranda was carrying were not a security threat, and so his detention was an abuse of press freedom. The middle ground was occupied by the view that 'prior censorship is necessary for some matters of national security'. The other end housed arguments from the right-wing press about the 'treasonable' nature of some of the leaks. There were several attacks directed at the *Guardian* for its 'irresponsibility' (for broader implications, see Chapter 7).

Germany

A dominant theme in the German media debate was the use and misuse of surveillance and other digital technologies as political instruments. In particular, the debate evolved from two core insights: that everyone is a victim of the NSA bulk surveillance and that national and transnational politics have no mechanism to legally put an end to NSA-style mass surveillance. The debate was also characterised by immense disappointment with the US breach of trust when it was revealed that they had been spying on Chancellor Angela Merkel's mobile phone. Consequently, a major part of the discussion concerned international relations and commented on how Germany should respond to the US. As the debate developed, newspapers increasingly highlighted current and future political and economic challenges related to media technologies, such as creating new technology markets or raising issues of media literacy as a key task for citizens to adopt to new realities, both on a European and national level.

Thus, at the beginning of the debate, ethical and normative questions played a key role. The NSA case signified a sudden and surprising threat to previously well-protected values of privacy. At the heart of the NSA scandal in the German discussion was the lack of respect towards citizen privacy rights, which was condemned as immoral. The domestic focus continued throughout summer 2013, when the German intelligence service step-by-step admitted its cooperation with the NSA. A major issue was how to define US–German relations in the future. It became paramount to determine what the American position was concerning spying on allies. By mid-December 2013, focus shifted to legal processes prompted by the revelations in Germany and the US.

Politicians and civil society figures were prominent in German outlets covering the story. Sources included established civil society interest groups, data protection activists, technology experts, and concerned citizens. Discussion on whistle-blowing was contributed not merely by German activists and journalists, but also by global actors involved in the case, such as Snowden, Greenwald, and WikiLeaks figure Julian Assange. German media raised questions about policy designs for internet governance and regulation, and called for European solutions (for broader implications, see Chapter 9).

France

The initial reaction to the Snowden revelations in France was a strong demand for legal oversight and calls for laws that would regulate digital surveillance. This was often suggested at the national level, but in the French debate the arguments for transnational rules were also put forth strongly. The revelations also provoked a specifically European discourse about the need for the continent to develop a global industrial strategy on media technology: Europe was encouraged to take advantage of the poor cyber civil rights reputations of the US, Russia, and China and offer an alternative policy. In this sense, the reference point in the French debate was not merely France but also Europe.

The debate also highlighted the necessity to bolster legal protection for journalists and their sources. These arguments often were linked to calls to provide asylum to Snowden and overlapped with demands for greater government transparency, an argument made for instance in a joint opinion piece by Julian Assange and Christophe Deloire in *Le Monde*. The revelations also provoked concerns about surveillance threatening institutional and professional boundaries of trust. Finally, a number of commentators viewed the incident through the lens of international politics, as an issue of diplomacy and power among the nations involved.

In France, the image of the ordinary citizen also figured in the debate – albeit much less than other actors. In particular, there were arguments calling for more media literacy, emphasising the need for citizens to be more aware of the extent to which their digital practices expose them to surveillance. Such arguments advocated for free software, new encryption techniques and often portrayed hackers and whistle-blowers as models of contemporary citizenship. The most active and visible contributors to the opinion pieces were journalists, followed by academics and public intellectuals. Experts from civil society and the private sector contributed some views, as did various civil servants, while contributions from major politicians and intelligence community representatives were minimal.

The debate, during 2013 and 2014, turned out to be exceptional in comparison to what came before and after (see Chapter 8). At the early stage, there were no lively public disagreements, but mostly a momentary consensus on the need to monitor surveillance. The debate largely focused on particular professional jurisdictions and on technicalities. Professionals of the intelligence community remained outside of this debate, and politicians involved in the debate were relatively discreet. This changed later, in the aftermath of a series of Paris terrorist attacks. The attacks brought legislative activity to the forefront and politicians skilfully argued for an urgent upgrade to the country's surveillance capabilities. A legal framework for surveillance was repeatedly presented as the precondition for effective monitoring. Thus, the question was not about whether surveillance was morally acceptable but whether it was legal. (For the implications of the French debate, see Chapter 6.)

China

The Chinese debate on digital surveillance was dominated by analysis of international politics and particularly its effects on the Sino-US relationship. The discussion emphasised the sensitive nature of China's position as an emerging power actor. On the one hand, the debate acknowledged the need to maintain a good relationship with the US. On the other hand, deep resentment was expressed about how China is frequently criticised by the US regarding its human rights records, restraints on freedom of speech, and the 'Great Fire Wall' on the internet. The NSA event, then, seemed to provide an ideal case for China to manage its relationship with the US by blaming the US for applying double standards. The commentaries under this theme generally criticised US hegemony, while defending and legitimising China's position.

Another major frame concerned internet technology and governance. A particular bargaining chip in the economic and technological competition with the US was the regulation of surveillance and, in this context, China was described as more effective and also more ethical. However, as will be discussed in Chapter 7, the NSA event was reported prominently in the Chinese media only in the first few weeks. This was also the time when Snowden was based in Chinese territory, Hong Kong. With his leaving for Russia, the amount of reporting on the event in general dropped significantly. Today, over three years after Snowden's first revelation, his name and a series of issues attached to his revelation are only scantly mentioned in the mainstream Chinese media.

A less prominent theme was a highlighting of the reaffirmation of Hong Kong's 'democratic' reputation. This interpretation emerged in the early phase of the revelations, when Snowden was based in Hong Kong. Since its return to China's sovereignty in the late 1990s, Hong Kong society – and the international community – has been heavily concerned about the fate of democracy in the region. The Chinese government has been regularly criticised for the limitations it has imposed on Hong Kong's ability to function as a democracy (deterioration of press freedom, implementation of nationalist education). In this context, the Chinese government and its officially sanctioned opinion coverage was keen to argue that Hong Kong is still democratic, although in its own way. Snowden's choice of Hong Kong as the site to publish the revelations served as evidence for the Chinese government to reaffirm a democratic Hong Kong to the international public.

Hong Kong newspapers framed the event within Sino-US relations, but combined it with Hong Kong–US relations. The reluctance of China to actively handle the Snowden incident in Hong Kong was described in the media as understandable. The interpretation saw it as evidence that, for pro-China voices in Hong Kong, the most important aspect of handling Snowden was to avoid China's direct confrontation with the

US. Media reactions in Hong Kong included opinions that aggressively argued for China's necessity to bolster its self-defence. They also urged China to forge a stronger alliance with Russia and Europe in opposition to the US. Overall, opinion pieces often concluded that the Snowden incident would give the upper hand to China vis-à-vis the US on the issues of internet security. Nevertheless, many also believed that the Snowden incident was merely a small episode in Sino-US relations that would not and should not influence the more general 'great power relationship' between the two countries.

The concern over Hong Kong–US relations rested mainly in fear that the US would take revenge on Hong Kong, for example, by denying visa-free access to Hong Kong passport holders. The Hong Kong government's decision, however, to allow Snowden to leave rather than extraditing him back to the US betrayed no such fear. Many contributors in the media lauded this decision as the best way to protect Hong Kong's interests. It helped solve the immediate political crisis before any possible political interventions by China and the Hong Kong government. The Snowden–NSA incident obviously strained Hong Kong–US relations. After Snowden's revelations in Hong Kong, many media, political figures, and civic groups demanded an apology from the US. They suggested that NSA's surveillance in Hong Kong was unnecessary and illegitimate because it was inconceivable that Hong Kong would constitute a base of terrorism that would necessitate US monitoring.

As Snowden appeared in Hong Kong, the pro-China politicians and media accused the pro-democracy camp (mainly the *Apple Daily*) of not defending Hong Kong vocally enough against US surveillance. For them, this proved a patron–client relationship between the pro-democracy camp and US government. To counter-attack, the pro-democracy camp pointed to the establishment's hypocrisy: keeping silent on the internet control in China. This is an essential difference from mainland China, where national politics was untouched by the Snowden scandal. Also, in Hong Kong, it was more common than in mainland China to discuss whether Snowden was a hero or a traitor, a whistle-blower or a criminal, and whether the NSA's programmes were necessary, legitimate, and effective. Perhaps because Hong Kong – as Snowden revealed – has long been the 'victim' of US surveillance, public opinion sided with Snowden. Even those who believed in the necessity of global surveillance often claimed that they were surprised by the scale and scope of the NSA activities.

Russia

The initial reaction to the NSA scandal in Russia sparked discussion about the relations between the US, the EU, China, Russia, and also the role of Latin American states (that were at that time considered potential final destinations for Snowden). As the popular daily *Moskovskij Komsomolets* titled one of its early stories, 'Snowden's escape is a slap in Washington's face by Moscow and Beijing' (*MK*, 26 June 2013).

Another prominent theme developed was the normalisation of spying, seeing surveillance as a standard practice of national defence and a means for protecting strategic geopolitical and economic interests. In this respect, Russian media discussed the NSA scandal as a problem of modern intelligence work that paradoxically becomes more and more transparent, exposing the internal routines of state agencies. This happens due to the proliferation of digital technologies that not only help to gather intelligence but also make it easier to access documents and databases.

As a solution to this crisis of intelligence work, and to a number of other security-related issues, the theme of internet governance and the need to reform media and information legislation came to the forefront of the Russian debate. A typical example of how these themes developed appears in the headline of a *Moskovskij Komsomolets* article that posed the question: 'Will Merkel take the internet and Google away from the Americans?' (*MK*, 18 February 2014). The text opens with a short factual statement that the German Chancellor suggested building a new communication infrastructure in Europe in order to bypass the US-controlled internet hubs (For the implications of the Russian debate, see Chapter 8.)

* * *

As noted earlier, one clear variable of domestication was the level of national involvement in the NSA intelligence networks and the relative geopolitical position of respective countries. It follows that, in the US and UK, the event was not merely about foreign affairs. The Snowden–NSA event was also seen through the lens of domestic political accountability. In France and Germany, the discussion set out as a more general critique of the use of mass surveillance, told from the perspective of victims of surveillance. As the debate developed, the involvement of respective states was gradually disclosed, which brought new elements to the legitimate controversy. In Russia, China, and Hong Kong, the key terms of public debate were also drawn from the national regimes of power, while using the exposure of digital surveillance as a criticism of the US. Unlike in France and Germany, this was not spelled out as criticism of the state but it rather supported Russian and Chinese security institutions.

The work of legitimation: three principles

Arguments in the public debate do not merely point to particular political views. They also act to justify proposed courses of action. In analysing the rhetoric and discursive strategies supporting public arguments of the NSA debate, we draw inspiration from the work of French sociologists Luc Boltanski and Laurent Thévenot (2006). In their theory of justification, public arguments have a core moral structure: in order to convince opponents in political disagreements, speakers need to evoke some higher principle or social value acknowledged by all parties. From this perspective, any public controversy can offer material from which to detect principles that are culturally and politically available and legitimate. The NSA revelations provide an opportunity to take stock of the contradictory ways in which the tensions between privacy and security were publicly resolved.

Initially, Boltanski and Thévenot identified six worlds of justification as means of resolving disputes. These relate to the principles of market, industry, home, civic life, fame, and inspiration. Each of these principles is *historically constructed* and rooted in distinct and canonised social theories. While the worlds of justification are rooted in a tradition of intellectual governance of modern societies, their uses in contemporary disputes must take distinct situations into account. Thus, there is interplay between the inherited established grammar of justification and the new conditions in which we live – such as the global, material realities, and contradictions related to digital surveillance. New principles may be crafted for making sense of how digital surveillance relates to security or privacy.

Intensive moments of attention to particular problems, or disruptive, unpredictable (media) events can sometimes serve as dramatic turning points where the existing balance between principles of justification can begin to be reworked. In this sense, media events can become *historical* – or transformative (see Chapter 1) – if the ensuing debates lead to changes and modifications in the deeper structure of justification discourse.

Whether such transformations take place is of course a question we can answer only in the long run.

Analysing the opinion pieces on the NSA revelations in 2013–14, we identified three principles evoked across national debates. By discussing these three – *political realism*, *balance*, and *transparency* – we will try to map out some of the key dynamics that have so far been in play in the surveillance debate.

Political realism

Within the *political realism* principle, digital surveillance is perceived as a naturalised part of the power game between nations. This justification relies on a materialistic and strategic view of power and disregards all other views as idealistic, naïve, and essentially unrealistic. In the international system, the argument goes, the political order will only stem from the assumption that nations recognise each other as calculating and self-interested actors. In this view, the political world is competitive and dangerous, and therefore the paternalistic guardianship of the state is necessary and justified. In times of peace and tranquillity, it may stand back but, in times of emergency, the state can legitimately intervene. Thus, in regard to security, the fundamental interests of the people and the state merge. The sovereignty and authority of the state, in other words, are necessary conditions for sovereignty of the citizenry.

Against this backdrop, Snowden's revelations constituted a moment of volatility. One central argument of political realism was that secret surveillance programmes have been developed and applied by security agencies the world over, and that there is simply no way to deny this fact. This viewpoint was succinctly expressed by guest *Wall Street Journal* contributor L. Gordon Crovitz, former publisher of the paper:

> Snowden's leaks left the false impression that the US is violating international norms, when in fact every major country has similar electronic monitoring services. China and Russia are strong competitors to the NSA. Former French Foreign Minister Bernard Kouchner corrected the record: 'Everyone is listening to everyone else. But we don't have the same means as the US, which makes us jealous.' (Wall Street Journal, 4 November 2013)

Echoing the same principle, an editorial in the German newspaper *Süddeutsche Zeitung* pointed out that not only does everyone spy, but that the widespread cooperation with the NSA undercuts any claim to moral authority: 'Moral outrage of countries that were spied on is hypocritical, too, as we know that Germany and France have cooperated with the NSA' (31 October 2013). Many pieces, like the one in the *Daily Telegraph*, reassured readers that the secret programmes 'should be a cause for comfort rather than concern' (8 June 2013); while a *New York Times* editorial lamented that the disclosure of clandestine surveillance undermined other political efforts:

> *Internationally all governments practice electronic surveillance, but the very scale of America's clandestine electronic operations appears to be undercutting America's soft power – its ability to influence global affairs through example and moral leadership.* (*New York Times*, 22 October 2013)

Political realism often links with assumptions about identity – who is to be protected and from whom – which are closely tied to patriotism. In the UK, many commentators in the surveillance debate justified the actions of intelligence agencies because these institutions are patriotic by default.

> *That the NSA and GCHQ should share such information ought to be a cause of comfort rather than concern. They don't gather information for the sake of it – they do it to keep us safer.* (*Daily Telegraph*, 8 June 2013)

The strong link between patriotism and political realism helps shed light on how interpretations outside the US and UK were mostly critical of digital surveillance. As they were focusing exclusively on the US, commentators in Russia and China were able to condemn spying on users of digital platforms. At the same time – following the same formal logic of realism as the *Daily Telegraph* above – they worked to legitimise strong domestic state control. An excerpt from the Chinese coverage demonstrates that political realism may not exclusively refer to the interest of the nation-state but can also draw support from cultural and religious traditions, which distinguish 'us' from 'them'. This enables the piece to simultaneously craft two forms of political realism: the seemingly cynical attitude of the US, and the serenity of China.

> *The way the US government officials handled the 'Snowden case' shows their usual ways of talking black into white and occupying the moral high ground for their own benefits. However, deeply influenced by the*

*Confucian culture, the Chinese people do believe in 'temperate, kind,
courteous, restrained and magnanimous diplomacy' and emphasise
that tolerance makes greatness.* (Global Times, 13 July 2013)

The core argument tied to political realism acted as a strong undercurrent
in much of the debate. On one end of the spectrum, politics was
viewed as timeless or almost static: nations will always aim to protect
themselves and pursue their interest by any means available. Moments of
political success or failure are transient. On the other end, the emphasis
was on the volatility of politics, where every political move matters and
each of them may have direct consequences for the security and success
of nations.

Ultimately, such realism makes politics a question of identity and
builds a public discourse that works to legitimise surveillance and state
action on the basis of a distinction between the state and its enemies (or
competitors). This position can cast conscientious citizens as traitors. For
journalism and journalists, it poses a complex challenge to professional
autonomy. On the one hand, it speaks forcefully to the 'realist' streak
associated with journalism, where reporters and editors nurture suspicion
of light-headed idealism. On the other hand, as concern for *security* pulls
at the realist reporter, it can erode commitments to professional autonomy.
If privacy is deemed a secondary value to security, also the privacy
of journalism–source relations can increasingly become a target of
surveillance, a threat faced by journalists working in varied systems all
over the world. When the borderline between *deviance* and *legitimate
controversy* is policed by mobilising a security-driven political realism,
journalism can find itself in narrowing – or at least more polarised –
national ideological spaces. With its realist underpinnings, there is a
danger that journalism, to whatever degree knowingly or unknowingly,
strengthens this trend.

Balance

The principle of *balance* colours the controversy in a way that regards
political power as a potentially destabilising element in society. It
manifests in the US as the separation of powers outlined in the
Constitution. Balance of power is seen as being achieved through
deliberate political decisions and therefore supports faith in rationality of
politics. Abuses of power can be prevented by intelligently designed

democracy. The principle betrays an optimism about the efficacy of the current systems, a feeling that, despite problems related to digital surveillance, the system can be patched up and made again to function smoothly and fairly.

In this respect, the biggest consequence of the NSA revelation was the potential or alleged breakdown of trust in the system. This concern was often articulated as questions about the health of the machinery of government preceding the exposure. Were politicians and institutions responsible for monitoring the intelligence agencies aware of the NSA practices? Did elected officials simply accept that the government could collect private data practically in any way they found necessary? Even more prominently, discussion on these lines explored ways to re-establish proper, confidence-building oversight.

The discourse about balance of power and oversight was, from the beginning, a dominant part of the US debate. The strong constitutional legacy of instituting checks and balances provided frequently opposing views on whether the system was functioning effectively. An editorial in the *Wall Street Journal* contended that the harm done by surveillance was exaggerated.

We bow to no one in our desire to limit government power, but data-mining is less intrusive on individuals than routine airport security. The data sweep is worth it if it prevents terror attacks that would lead politicians to endorse far greater harm to civil liberties. (Wall Street Journal, 7 June 2013)

The *New York Times*, on the other hand, suggested several times that the paradigm of oversight had been seriously damaged, but the suggestions usually came accompanied with an optimistic note pointing to a potential system fix. A belief in the relevance of the eighteenth-century language of the US Constitution to provide a functional blueprint for the digital era was still strong. A specific characteristic in the US debate was – at least in the early stages – the question of whether there is enough oversight to properly monitor the surveillance of *American* citizens.

While the principle of political realism valued surveillance for its necessity and efficacy, the discourse in the name of balance raised issues about political representation and due process. The viability of these arguments varied in different national settings. In the UK, the Snowden revelations led to a lively debate on political oversight and privacy. In the early months, contributing writers politely asked the government to provide convincing testimony on how intelligence agencies were being held accountable. A *Daily Telegraph* writer suggested that a detailed transparency policy would render institutional reforms unnecessary: 'explaining more of what [GCHQ] does would not limit its capabilities' (11 June 2013). The *Guardian* demanded more direct government oversight:

> *They [British parliamentarians] need to use their powers – they are there to be used – to probe and question the agencies and the oversight regime. They need to understand better, because Britain, like the US, needs a better balance between security and liberty in an era transformed by technologies most politicians barely know exist.* (*Guardian*, 29 October 2013)

German commentators were also explicit in their calls for an oversight fix. Interestingly, the European Union served here as an element in the argument for a *transnational* oversight mechanism. The German public discourse clearly regarded European proposed solutions as better and presumably more effective and credible than national ones. A news commentary in *Süddeutsche Zeitung* advocated for more protection of Europe's distinct traditions around privacy:

> *There is a necessity for a European Convention regarding secret services. Europe should organise political institutions and companies to create technology that operates in line with their understanding of privacy and security. This would bolster Europe's independence from the US.* (*Süddeutsche Zeitung*, 23 January 2014)

Calls for oversight were less dominant in Russia, where the scandal purportedly did not explicitly concern its own institutions. The legal limits of Russian domestic surveillance, however, were used as evidence of how the arrangements in Russia were working better than in the West:

> *In the context of the fight against international terrorism it [surveillance] becomes global and, on the whole, such methods are needed. ... It is all right when kept within the law that regulates the work of specialised services. It is bad when done outside the law. And [Putin] reiterated that wire-tapping without a court order is not allowed in Russia.* (*Kommersant Vlast*, 1 June 2013)

In the Chinese commentaries, international relations were the dominant concern. The debate emphasised the diversity of political and legal systems. The English-language *Global Times* ran an editorial arguing that domestic and international surveillance are two very different things. Where domestic surveillance lies in the jurisdiction of national legal systems, international surveillance should adhere to international norms:

> *American politicians just do not understand, or simply do not want to admit it, and they stick to their own legal systems, legal concepts and enforcement measures to deal with international affairs and related issues that are meant to be internal affairs of other countries. They totally disregard international influence and other countries' feelings.* (*Global Times*, 13 July 2013)

If one thinks about the role of journalism in the surveillance debate, the importance of defending the balance principle becomes a central issue. The notion of balance tied to oversight, at least in the short run, frames the debate about surveillance by *linking* professional autonomy to consequential systemic power and political institutions. If the terrain of political realism invites journalism into a potentially weak position, the terrain of balance at least tries to tie *political* power into questions of legitimation where journalism carries more rhetorical power. Political power can be, at least in a performative sense, tied to it. And while not overtly dominant in the debate, the principle of oversight has produced tangible consequences in terms of court decisions, policy reforms, and legal adjustments. The issue of surveillance and security, of course, raises the question of whether political power can – with the help of journalism – bring the security sector of the state under democratic oversight. This question, then, begins to overlap with the principle of transparency.

Transparency

Applied to the case of surveillance, transparency as a principle relies on the vague promise of the power of *revelation*. Exposing the mass-scale intrusion of state apparatuses into the realm of personal life taps into a source of spontaneous morality, which is compatible with assumptions about modern individualism. The roots of transparency discourse can be derived from the premise that 'maximum transparency contributes to maximal happiness' (Baume and Papadopoulos, 2015). This unabashedly optimistic understanding of transparency was introduced for instance in the early nineteenth century by utilitarian philosopher Jeremy Bentham. While this radical liberal argument was never fully embraced by democratic political systems, it has generally gained ground recently (Schudson, 2015) and been championed by cyber-dissident organisations, such as WikiLeaks and Anonymous (Coleman, 2014).

In the debates on the Snowden revelations, the principle of transparency was strongly pushed forward to justify the initial act of making public the leaked material. The global attention and the volume of the debate itself served as evidence that the disclosures were doing what Snowden intended, making the secret programmes visible, spurring public debate, and demanding reactions. When questioned by the UK Home Office Committee in December 2013, Alan Rusbridger of the *Guardian* articulated this view by listing people with high institutional status who subscribe to the same principle:

> *The roll call of people who have said there needs to be a debate about this includes three Presidents of the United States, two Vice-Presidents, generals ... the security chiefs in the US are all saying this a debate that in retrospect we know that we had to have. ... There are members of the House of Lords, people who have been charged with oversight of the security measures here. The former chair of the intelligence and security committee, Tom King, said this was a debate that had to be had and they had to review the laws. The director of national intelligence in the US said these were conversations that needed to happen. So in terms of the public interest, I don't think anyone is seriously questioning this.* (*Guardian*, 3 December 2013)

Arguments for transparency were also key to discussions on the legitimacy of whistle-blowing. In the ensuing debates, the principle of transparency was often omitted, as the attention was paid to whether or not Snowden was an appropriate messenger, a genuine whistle-blower, a hero or traitor (Qin, 2015). Many interpretations in the media testified to Snowden's unselfishness, which indirectly perhaps justifies transparency as noble and ethically objective by default.

> *Snowden has proven to be a genuine whistle-blower, as he has not benefited from the leaking of information but rather suffered from it*

personally. He has acted out of a pure sense of morality, therefore is the very model of a refugee [eligible for political asylum]. (Süddeutsche Zeitung, 2 November 2013)

The principle of transparency also lent support to arguments about people's right to know. In this context, the articulations of the transparency were often intimately attached to the discourse of balance. In this sense, transparency helped to explain why political oversight of intelligence agencies is necessary.

In a democracy, people are entitled to know what techniques are being used by the government to spy on them, how the records are being held and for how long, who will have access to them, and the safeguards in place to prevent abuse. Only then can they evaluate official claims that the correct balance between fighting terrorism and preserving individual liberty has been struck, and decide if they are willing to accept diminished privacy and liberty. (New York Times, 11 June 2013)

While the principles of political realism and balance almost exclusively highlighted the role of the state, transparency was also connected to the market. The most prominent articulation of this connection came in the public standoff between intelligence agencies and internet service providers. The companies became vocal defenders of transparency. Their initiatives for greater transparency were greeted with applause, most notably by technological experts and niche publications, as the following passage in an article from the Verge demonstrates:

Over two dozen companies and a number of trade groups have signed a letter supporting bills that would let them reveal more details about the government's secret information requests. ... Apple, Google, Microsoft, Facebook, and Yahoo all signed the letter, as did the Software Alliance and the Internet Association, a lobbying group founded by Google, eBay, and others. These aren't just big names in the tech world, they're also the companies that were named as contributing data to the PRISM surveillance program – and the ones that have been fighting back against secrecy restrictions. All four of the aforementioned companies have suits pending against the US government, arguing that being unable to tell users how many requests have been received and complied with violates their right to free speech. (Verge, 30 September 2013)

Following the long tail of this debate, the role of technology companies shows the increasing cultural currency of the value or principle of transparency (see Schudson, 2015). As a reaction to the NSA disclosures, technology companies have prolifically raised the number of personal encryption choices available to their customers. In the spring of 2016, a legal stalemate between global internet and communications giants and US security agencies began heating up when federal investigators demanded that companies help blur such boundaries. It is too early to tell how this will turn out, but Mike Masnick of the blog *Techdirt* identified interesting emerging alliances in the media sphere:

> The Wall Street Journal editorial board, which is notoriously pro-surveillance, has come out with an editorial that argues that Apple is right on encryption and should resist the FBI's demands. ... This is the same WSJ that published an editorial calling Ed Snowden a sociopath and arguing for less oversight of the NSA. ... On its own the WSJ piece is a nice summary of the issue. However, given the source, it's absolutely amazing. It suggests that, even among its usual allies, the DOJ's [Department of Justice] arguments in favour of backdooring encryption are not working very well. (*Techdirt*, 3 March 2016)

As the excerpts above suggest, the debate on transparency appeared much thinner in mainstream newspapers than in blogs specialising on digital technology. In addition, opinionated journalism tended to be even more distant from academic discussions, which have addressed the ambiguity of transparency. A typical unambiguous argument is that 'clarity obtained through information [is] a direct path to accountability and good governance' (Flyverbom, 2015: 168–9).

The fact that the debate following the Snowden revelations has made some governments and experts think about 'transparency of surveillance' (e.g. Anderson, 2015: 8) or in a more half-hearted spirit about 'translucency' (Hayden, 2016: 422–4) may be somewhat paradoxical. Yet the Snowden revelations demonstrate how the recently emerged culture of digital leaks has empowered journalism, crafting a new kind of potential. Whether – and in what cases – the revelatory, watchdog power of journalism leads to an articulation of transnational publics that apply consequential pressure to policy choices remains to be seen. At minimum, what is at stake is the legitimacy of journalism to act in this capacity.

Domestication and transnationalism revisited

The public debates on digital surveillance prompted by Snowden's revelations were powerfully domesticated. They were strongly shaped and dominated by national constellations of power. This is not surprising. Domestication is an important tool in the work of informing national publics about global and transnational events and issues that lie outside direct experience. In addition, domestication paves the way to public debates that connect questions of international origin to national policy-making and the contestation of political power. In a more abstract sense, national public debates fostered by domestication contribute to 'global debates' on the same topics. While there is no shared platform where all participants could engage in dialogue, there is awareness of, and sometimes overlap with, debates taking place elsewhere.

Given that the political and cultural contexts vary from one country to another, it is obvious that strong practices of domestication yield different interpretations of the same event in mainstream journalism around the globe. Most explicitly – almost self-evidently – national debates were constrained (in both their volume and diversity) by the political systems in which the national media platforms are embedded. In Russia and China the state policing of mainstream media and civil society effectively denied mainstream interpretations that might have helped to raise questions about need for domestic oversight of their own states' surveillance activities. This, of course, does not mean that such views and demands would not exist in these countries, but the political and cultural resources available (in 2013–14) were not there to underscore the contradictions that existed between the rhetoric of criticising the US-led surveillance apparatus and the actual domestic practices of control.

On the other hand, pointing out this obvious discrepancy should not obscure the fact that Western countries too strongly defended state surveillance. In the UK and US, the defence frequently took place in mainstream media, often splitting the field politically – not between old-fashioned right and left, but rather between positions of national-patriotic power realism and those more sceptical of state power (both from left and right). In these debates, as in China and Russia, political realism and patriotic duties could be forged into a powerful arguments in support of effective mass surveillance (see also Chapters 3 and 4). What differentiates China and Russia from the UK and US, in this respect, is the ability of some journalists and other public actors to evoke questions about legitimacy of state power and trust in its institutions in general. Clearly, however, new geopolitical arrangements raise new questions about how the relationships between journalism, the public and the state are ordered and organised in the current global conjuncture. On one hand, we see at least momentarily empowered journalism that can take advantage of the transnational conditions and events – this is the abstract democratic promise incorporated in the intersection between digital leak culture and transnational (elite) journalism. On the other hand, our French analysis (Chapter 5) also demonstrates how contingent events, such as the terror attacks of 2015, can produce conditions where dominant discourse about security powerfully marginalises calls to protect civil rights.

Despite strong domestication, the NSA debate also has a decidedly transnational character. Partly this was the case because the revelations engaged national governments – including their heads of state personally – in changing and contradictory roles in the flow of discussion. Countries that first expressed outrage at US spying – such as Germany and France – turned out to be involved in it themselves. Governments that seemed to appreciate Snowden's action – such as China and Russia – could not wholly embrace his message and supported only distorted versions of its meaning and associations. These, and other similar discrepancies, left official speakers in positions that were at least potentially vulnerable to criticism. Thus, not only were public commentators aware of their opponents in their national spheres of controversy but they also had to situate their arguments in an imagined space that cut across such borders. The fact that there is no clearly designated 'space' in which such global discourse could take place does not mean that it is non-existent. This is what makes the analysis of the production of legitimation worthwhile.

The main principles of *political realism, balance,* and *transparency* discussed above do not exhaustively describe the terrain of the debate, but they provide an overview of some of the dominant assumptions manifest in the debate, including assumptions about the role of journalism. According to the political realism justification, journalists and their sources are easily seen as a threat. However, political realism may appear attractive and professionally rewarding for journalists, as it is anchored in critical thinking suspicious of political demagoguery and naïve idealism. In debates on international politics and security policies, it may draw support from patriotism and national populism as well as from subtle forms of methodological nationalism (Beck, 2006). These perspectives may help the domestication of international and global events, as these can be perceived as 'business as usual'. This means that political realism does not prepare journalists to look for new or emergent features in the world of politics.

For those who argue for institutional balance, journalism is a tool in the process of legitimations. While the principle of balance is more optimistic about the possibility of reform, it may reinforce another version of 'business as usual' in politics. It situates the debates and concerns about the legitimacy of surveillance in the realm of institutional politics. This would suggest that questions of oversight belong to two chambers of elites: those who are supposed to design policies (politicians and experts), and those who observe these processes at a distance (elite newspapers and their readers).

In the transparency justification, journalists are an essential part of the process of exposing and monitoring institutions of political power. Indeed, the principle of transparency highlights the role of advocacy journalism exemplified by Glenn Greenwald, Laura Poitras, and some members of the *Guardian* staff reporting the Snowden stories. In addition, it points to the increasing fragmentation of institutional journalism and its hybridisation. As Andrew Chadwick (2013) notes, at the heart of the transition is not a replacement of mainstream journalism and large media organisations, but their increasing adaptation to new practices and professional ideologies. Due to its vague articulations and perhaps treacherous implications for political life, transparency can hardly be the prime mover in the development of journalism. Nonetheless, it seems that the Snowden revelations helped move it into public debate.

Identifying both nation-specific strategies for legitimations and 'quasi-universal' transnational principles for justification, we can more clearly understand how domestic justifications feed into transnational discourses, forming a sort of global debate. Taken as a whole, the discourses mapped here account for the various geopolitical and media realities that shaped different strands of debate, and in the case of the principle of transparency, even hint at where the debate might be headed. Taking stock of these meanings is an ongoing process that will continue as we come to terms with the global digital environment and one that will raise key questions about ongoing negotiations of privacy, citizenship, and the role of journalism.

Note

1   The Fourth Amendment of the US Constitution provides, '[t]he right of the people to be secure in their persons, houses, papers, and effects, against unreasonable searches and seizures, shall not be violated, and no warrants shall issue, but upon probable cause'. https://www.law.cornell.edu/constitution/fourth_amendment.

3

Justifying Surveillance: The New Discursive Settlement in UK Opinionated Journalism

Karin Wahl-Jorgensen and Katy Jones

The UK media played a unique role in the revelations exposed by Edward Snowden regarding NSA mass surveillance programmes. The classified documents were first revealed to journalist Glenn Greenwald and were subsequently published in the *Guardian*, which continued to provide high-volume coverage of the story over a prolonged period of time. Following the initial revelations, discussion of several related incidents appeared in the *Guardian* as well as other mainstream news publications.

This chapter examines the distinctive discourses on the NSA revelations in the opinionated journalism of British newspapers, based on a qualitative analysis of a series of case studies following the initial Snowden leaks. The chapter demonstrates that, despite the key role of the *Guardian* in facilitating the revelations, British newspaper discourses overwhelmingly contributed to legitimating practices of mass surveillance. These justifications for surveillance were framed with reference to concerns about national security, but frequently accompanied and softened by pleas for increased transparency regarding the nature and extent of surveillance. As the chapter also shows, however, discussion of the revelations was informed by the politically polarised nature of the British newspaper landscape, with significant differences between the opinions voiced in right-leaning and left-leaning newspapers, which also occasioned a broader discussion of the boundaries of journalism, through criticism and defence of the *Guardian's* role in the revelations.

If there is a 'reshuffle in the perception of the world stemming from a quick shift from one regime to another' (Boltanski and Thévenot, 2006:

363), the British coverage of the NSA leaks implies that the reshuffle represents a new settlement based on the normalisation of surveillance – however uneasy and contested. This settlement is premised on the assumption that surveillance is a necessary evil that may be regulated and subjected to new forms of visibility. Through the discursive settlement, the necessity of surveillance is placed largely outside the sphere of legitimate controversy and pushed back into the sphere of consensus (Hallin, 1986).

Legitimating surveillance in the British press: conceptual framework

The British media system as a whole has typically been described as belonging to a 'liberal' or 'Anglo-American' model (e.g. Hallin and Mancini, 2004), characterised by (a) independence from political powers, (b) a control or watchdog function over political powers, (c) objectivity, (d) professional standards that reinforce the independence of journalism from other societal powers and professions, and (e) reporting functions that are distinct from those of comment and interpretation (Mancini, 2005). On the face of it, this suggests a media system that stands outside of ideological allegiances. The British newspaper landscape, however, remains distinctive in terms of its 'external pluralism' in the form of competing newspapers with distinctive ideological positions. Certainly, scholars who have carried out comparative research on journalism have noted the dominance of a sensational, negative, interpretative, and partisan press in Britain, with both 'low-end' and 'high-end' newspapers spread across the political spectrum (Esser and Umbricht, 2013: 991). A recent YouGov poll demonstrated that the British press is perceived as the most politically biased and right-wing in Europe (*Independent*, 7 February 2016).

For Chadwick and Collister, however, the *Guardian*'s action in publishing the revelations represented 'an important punctuating phase in the evolution of political journalism and political communication as media systems continue to adapt to the incursion of digital media logics' (2014: 2420). They suggest that the newspaper astutely navigated a swiftly changing technological landscape, maximising its organisational advantage by drawing on technological innovations such as Twitter livechats, liveblogging, linking, and the embedding of third-party content. Ultimately, they argued that the handling of the leaks showed how 'adaptive professional news organizations can successfully translate their power to shape politics and challenge state power' (ibid. 2435).

Despite this optimistic appraisal, it is also clear that both the *Guardian* and figures associated with the Snowden leaks in the UK paid a heavy price for their participation in the unfolding revelations. The newspaper not only faced extensive criticism from other media organisations, as will be discussed later in more detail, but also was ordered by the Government Communications Headquarters to destroy hard disks containing leaked information (Harding, 2014). Glenn Greenwald's partner, David Miranda, was subsequently detained by the British authorities in Heathrow Airport – an episode attracting significant coverage and debate. At the same time, while the *Guardian* played a central role in the revelations and published, along with other British newspapers, reports and commentaries critical of mass surveillance, the British coverage, including some *Guardian* commentary, was overwhelmingly focused on the legitimation of surveillance.

Method

We investigated discourses on surveillance after the NSA leaks through the selection of seven newspapers (and their weekend equivalents) that represent tabloid and quality publications, as well as different political stances and readerships (figures for average daily circulation are from the Audit Bureau of Circulations for January 2015):

- The *Guardian* is a national daily newspaper and has a large web presence. The paper identifies with centre-left liberalism and its readership is generally on the mainstream left of British political opinion. Average daily circulation: 185,429.
- The *Independent* is regarded as leaning to the left politically, making it primarily a competitor to the *Guardian*, even though it still features some conservative columnists and tends to take a classical liberal, pro-market stance on economic issues. Average daily circulation: 61,338.[1]
- The *Daily Telegraph* is a quality newspaper characterised by a traditionalist, centre-right political orientation. It consistently backs

the Conservative Party in UK elections (hence the nickname *Torygraph*). Average daily circulation: 494,675.

- *The Times* is a daily national newspaper considered to be traditionally a moderately centre-right newspaper. Its sister paper, the *Sunday Times*, occupies a dominant position in the quality Sunday market. Average daily circulation: 396,621.
- The *Daily Mail* is a daily middle-market tabloid newspaper, known for its right-leaning, pro-conservative, Eurosceptic stance. Average daily circulation: 1,688,727.
- The *Sun* is a daily national 'red top' tabloid newspaper and the biggest-selling newspaper in the UK. It is populist and right-leaning. Average daily circulation: 1,978,702.
- The *Daily Mirror* is a tabloid 'red top' newspaper. It has a left-leaning slant, and has consistently endorsed the Labour Party over the years. Average daily circulation: 992,235.

To make the sample manageable, we used a multi-step process in narrowing down our examination of key episodes following the Snowden leaks. We first constructed a newspaper timeline with the aid of the Nexis newspaper database, using 'Edward Snowden', as well as the names for the two main intelligence agencies implicated in the Snowden revelations, the 'NSA' and 'GCHQ', as search terms. The results of this timeline were then charted against the major episodes within the larger story of the leaks. These episodes were based upon timelines and resources created by the major news organisations and outlets covering the story. On that basis, four case studies, representing peaks in coverage that encapsulated key debates around surveillance, were chosen (see Figure 3.1):

1. Initial leaks: the initial revelations and Snowden's unveiling as the source of the leaks.
2. (a) Embassy snooping and (b) spying on world leaders: the interception of communications in foreign embassies and European Union offices, and spying on world leaders' phone communications, in particular German Chancellor Angela Merkel. These two have been combined to make a more comparative sample of articles.
3. The detention of journalist Glen Greenwald's partner David Miranda at Heathrow Airport under anti-terror legislation (Schedule 7).

4. The *Charlie Hebdo* terror attacks in Paris that prompted debates about digital encryption, freedom of speech, and the resurrection of the so-called 'Snoopers' Charter'.

Keyword searches, timeframes, and results

For each episode, we conducted a Nexis UK search with specific keywords and a timeframe corresponding to the episodes. The initial timeframe was a two-week period following each episode, but in the case of Episode 2b (spying on world leaders), the timeframe was extended to four weeks to provide a more robust sample, given the more dispersed timeline of coverage for this story. Opinionated texts were identified by the name of the section in the paper where the article appeared (i.e. opinion, comment, and editorial).

Given the fact that the *Guardian* was central to facilitating the revelations, it is unsurprising that it contained the largest number of articles across all episodes (34 out of 80). The quality press produced far more opinion pieces on the topic than the popular press throughout the entire sample period (65 and 15 respectively). While the quality press was most concerned with the initial leaks (37 out of 65 articles), the tabloid press produced the biggest number of opinion pieces following the detention of David Miranda (8 of 15 articles).

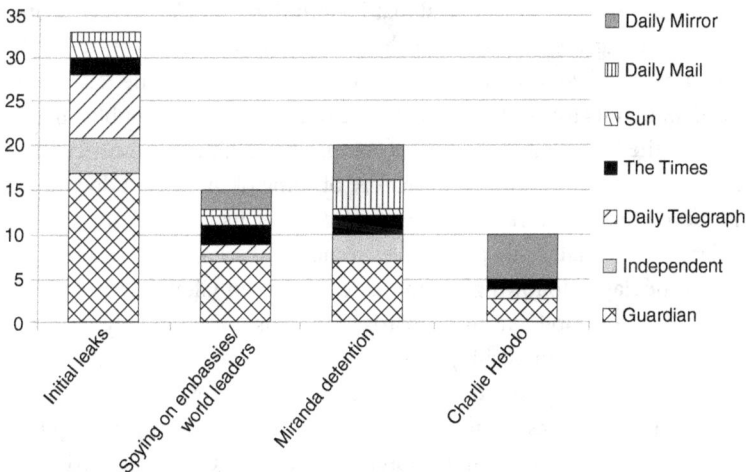

Figure 3.1   Distribution of opinion pieces by newspaper and episode (n = 80)

What emerges from our analysis is a clear pattern: an argument for the need for greater transparency, oversight and accountability around practices of mass surveillance is coupled with a justification of mass surveillance in the interest of national security.

Underpinning this debate is a particular theme which exposes the deeply politically heteronymous (Benson and Neveu, 2005: 5) and polarised nature of the journalistic field in Britain. While right-leaning newspapers are quick to criticise the *Guardian* and its role in facilitating the Snowden revelations, left-leaning publications were more likely to support the publication through arguments focusing on the freedom of the press. This demonstrates that, in the UK context, discussions over the Snowden revelations ultimately came to encapsulate not just a discussion over the trade-off between individual rights and national security, but also about press freedom, particularly following the detention of David Miranda. As such, the NSA leaks represented a meta-discussion over the boundaries of the journalistic profession and the responsibilities of the media (see Chadwick and Collister, 2014), but one which took place within an already-existing ideological battleground.

The polarised context: blaming the *Guardian*

The already-existing ideological battleground of the UK press shaped responses along the fault lines of the political spectrum. Here, the right-leaning *Sun* and *Mail* newspapers were quick to criticise the left-leaning *Guardian* and its associates for their role in facilitating and publishing the leaks, on the basis that their actions compromised national security. These debates stressed the 'treasonable' nature of some of the leaked documents, with several attacks directed at the *Guardian* for its 'irresponsible' role in the leaks, which allegedly posed risks to national security.

Immediately following the initial leaks, Steven Glover, writing in the *Daily Mail*, exemplified this polarisation. His piece openly criticised the *Guardian* for publishing the revelations, arguing that the action reflected an assumption that the 'British government has no right to defend British interests, and ultimately the security of the State' (*Daily Mail*, 18 June 2013). The implication here is that the *Guardian*'s actions are unpatriotic and fly in the face of national security concerns. Writing in the *Sun*, columnist and former Conservative member of Parliament Louise

Mensch further exemplified this position in an attack on the actions of the left-wing press – particularly the *Guardian* – and its alignment to Labour politicians:

> *When the Guardian screeched that Miranda was arrested just for being a journalist's partner, a mostly supine, lickspittle Press rowed in behind them – yelling about Press Freedom and smearing the names of our security forces at Heathrow, who were just doing their jobs. … Keen for at least a FEW good headlines in their Summer of Discontent, Shadow Home Secretary Yvette Cooper jumped on the Guardian's bandwagon – demanding an investigation, branding it an abuse of the Terrorism Act and calling for a review of our powers against the bad guys. Bad call, Yvette – very bad call. As Shadow Home Secretary you are auditioning for the big job. And band-wagon-jumping is not the way to go. Home Secretaries are meant to keep us safe. … Yvette pre-judged national security based on a Leftie newspaper.* (*Sun*, 25 August 2013, Episode 3)

Mensch's argument articulated an explicit ideological opposition to the *Guardian* as a 'leftie' paper which placed national security at risk, and sought to minimise concerns about press freedom as irrelevant in the broader context of keeping 'us safe'. Other pieces which condemned the *Guardian* also used the NSA revelations as an opportunity to raise questions about the responsibilities and jurisdictional boundaries (Schudson and Anderson, 2008) of the journalistic profession. As sociologists have demonstrated, professions claim exclusive jurisdiction over particular domains – or types of tasks – by linking knowledge claims convincingly to forms of daily work practice (e.g. Abbott, 1988). If the *Guardian*'s role in the NSA revelations represented a challenge to conventional boundaries of journalistic practice and enabled the newspaper to reconfigure and renew its power (Chadwick and Collister, 2014: 2420), this did not go uncontested in the right-wing press. Instead, some of the coverage critical of the newspaper pointed to the ways in which its actions contravened the expectations of journalists operating within a particular national context. A *Daily Mail* opinion piece suggested after the detention of David Miranda exemplified this line of argumentation:

> *The Guardian appears to have entered very dangerous waters where journalists who care for their country should not venture. … With friends*

> *like Edward Snowden and employees like Glenn Greenwald, that*
> *[damaging the country] is what the Guardian is in danger of doing.*
> (*Daily Mail*, 20 August 2013, Episode 3)

This article makes an interesting rhetorical move in generating the figure of 'journalists who care for their country'. This normalises the notion that news workers *simultaneously* inhabit their professional role and the role of a patriot. The former is characterised by impartiality, objectivity, and independence, the latter points to being partial to caring for one's country. Steven Glover's opinion piece about the initial NSA revelations, cited above, expanded further on the ways in which the newspaper had overstepped the boundaries of responsible journalism:

> *Even the BBC, which normally treats the Guardian as its house journal*
> *and guiding star, has so far not followed up the paper's latest overblown*
> *revelations with as much enthusiasm as might have been expected.*
> *Perhaps the Corporation can see that this is a story which tells us far*
> *more about the Guardian than anything else. Don't imagine the paper is*
> *being naïve: it is far too sophisticated for that. Treachery is too strong a*
> *word, but it is impossible to find any decent motive for what the Guardian*
> *has done. These supposedly world-shattering revelations were intended to*
> *damage the British government at the beginning of a crucial summit.*
> *More and more, it looks like a paper driven by its own obsessions,*
> *convinced only of its own virtue, which has simply lost the plot.* (*Daily*
> *Mail*, 18 June 2013, Episode 1)

For Glover, then, the story of the NSA leaks provides a meta-narrative about the uses and abuses of media power based on assumptions about the boundaries of journalism. Through this narrative, the *Guardian* is constructed as a news organisation which has become obsessed with its role as a player in national and global politics, to the point that it could be seen as guilty of treachery. This is precisely because the *Guardian* played an instrumental role in controlling the release of the story with the allegedly deliberate intention of harming the government. For these (largely right-leaning) critics, it seemed, the *Guardian* was violating normative expectations that newspapers, while independent, also have a responsibility to uphold national security to avoid damage to the government and, hence, the nation-state. This reveals a key tension in right-leaning newspapers' discourses on the role of journalism: on the one hand, newspapers should steer clear of acting as political actors in their own right when their actions might cause a threat to the plans of government. On the other hand, they have a responsibility to act as patriots.

By contrast, left-leaning newspapers were more likely to articulate concerns over censorship and restraints on press freedom, particularly in relation to the detention of David Miranda (Episode 3). Miranda's detention was justified by the UK government on the grounds that he was carrying material that 'could aid terrorism', which constitutes a 'threat to national security'. Papers including the *Guardian* and the *Independent*, however, rejected the claim that the documents Miranda was carrying could be a security threat, and instead suggested that his detention was a violation against press freedom:

> *There's no conceivable way copies of the Snowden revelations seized last week at Heathrow could aid terrorism or 'threaten the security of the British state' ... When the supposed monitors of the secret services merely parrot their jargon against press freedom, we should know this regime is not up to its job. ... As one official said in wielding his legal stick over the Guardian: 'You have had your debate. There's no need to write anymore.'*
> (*Guardian*, 20 August 2013, Episode 1)

The suggestion of an entrenched 'jargon against press freedom' highlights the ways in which arguments for surveillance contribute to the suppression of a free press. It ultimately offers a critique of the excessive use of security arguments to underpin the secret uses and abuses of power. The idea that intelligence services were acting excessively in their attempts at curbing press freedom was not articulated just in the *Guardian*, but was also given voice in the *Independent*.

> *[N]ational security must be paramount. But there are lines to be drawn – between the message and the medium, between Britain's interests and America's, between enforcement and intimidation.* (*Independent*, 21 August 2013, Episode 1)

Here, the criticism of the intelligence services is circumscribed by the insistence that 'national security must be paramount'. This calls attention to the ways in which a discourse of surveillance in the interest of national security has by and large been removed from the sphere of legitimate controversy and now firmly resides within the sphere of consensus (Hallin, 1986). As we will later discuss in more detail, this was, indeed, one of the most important overarching themes.

Overall, these examples demonstrate that the NSA revelations, as they played out in the British context, represented an opportunity to debate the boundaries of journalistic practice (occasionally within the context of discussing the similarly contentious boundaries of intelligence activity), and articulate the role of the *journalist as a responsible patriot*. At the same time, in discussing the role of the media, there appeared to be a resignation, across the political spectrum, to the idea that national security remains a powerful legitimation strategy and one that is difficult to trump with arguments for press freedom.

Transparency and the legitimation of surveillance

Informed by this backdrop of ideologically underpinned boundary work, the debates following the NSA revelations took a particular shape in the British press. Rather than being dominated by concerns about privacy and individual rights and liberties, the most prominent theme in opinionated coverage related to the need for transparency, oversight, and accountability around the extent and nature of surveillance. That is to say, instead of taking issue with acts of state surveillance in itself, these discourses raised questions about the *lack of transparency* regarding these acts (see also discussion of this issue in Chapter 2).

This emphasis could be seen as a natural extension of the prevailing 'Zeitgeist of transparency' (Stohl et al., 2016), signalling a broader trend in the 'growing demand for openness, transparency and accountability' (Wood and Wright, 2015). This 'triumph of transparency' (Braithwaite and Drahos, 2000) revolves around a belief in increased information and communication as a direct path to accountability, trust, and legitimacy (Garsten and de Montoya, 2008). The transparency literature often equates information with transparency and considers this clarity to be a direct path to accountability and good governance (Christensen and Cheney, 2015). Public discourses suggest that transparency will act as a 'disinfectant that will remove corruption, secrecy, and other kinds of misconduct' (Flyverbom et al., 2016: 102). Transparency is intrinsically and causally tied to accountability: 'Transparency ... is supposed to *generate* accountability, even though the exact process that leads from one to the other is not always clear' (Fox, 2007, quoted in Christensen and Cheney, 2015: 71). The emphasis on transparency should also be understood against the backdrop of longer standing public debates on the secrecy – and resulting abuses of power – of the UK's intelligence services (e.g. Gill, 2012).

Indeed, in our study, transparency emerged as a dominant theme across the first three episodes: the initial leaks, the snooping on world leaders and embassies, and the detention of David Miranda. The notion was first introduced in the context of avoiding a political cover-up by not allowing 'a cabal of grave-faced, middle-aged politicians and spies to bury this scandal' (*Guardian*, 8 June 2013, Episode 1). This was tied to a discourse surrounding the notion of trust (or lack of) in the state, suggesting that, without transparency from the state and agencies, the public cannot be expected to trust their actions:

> *Yet the tightrope between public confidence and public safety is one that must be walked. In an age when everybody has an e-mail address, it is not enough to simply ask the public to trust that all is well. Rather, they must be offered reasons to have faith in the oversight that keeps it so.* (*The Times*, 10 June 2013, Episode 1)

Such journalistic commentary reflects arguments put forward in the transparency literature: transparency puts greater responsibilities on the observed and, in order to have 'credibility and respect', the actions of organisations must be transparent (Oliver, 2004: 6). It has been argued, however, that this 'simple and deceptive formula' that correlates information with transparency, and leads directly to accountability, good governance, trust and legitimacy, 'conflates and simplifies a much more dynamic and complex relationship between transparency effort and organisational and regulatory effects' (Flyverbom, 2016: 119).

Though the emphasis on transparency was dominant across the sample and newspapers, there were subtle differences reflecting the political orientation amongst the newspapers. Right-leaning newspapers, including *The Times* and *Telegraph*, supported the idea of striking a balance between security and liberty. According to the positions they put forward, government must convince us why extra surveillance powers are needed because 'we' all know that clear intelligence is crucial for our security. These arguments were premised on the assumption that intelligence keeps us safe.

> *Ministers in Britain now need to make the case for why they need the extra powers they seek in the Data Communications Bill ... It would be naive to think that law enforcement agencies can combat terrorism without clear intelligence. ... That information is never handed over voluntarily. The authorities insist that a strictly legal framework is not violated. It is important to clarify that this is the case. The balance between security and freedom is delicate and its price is eternal vigilance.*
> (*The Times*, 8 June 2013, Episode 1)

Other commentators argued that we need a 'proper debate in parliament' and to be assured that the data is being obtained legally (*The Times*, 9 June 2013, Episode 1), and also to be given reasons why the Snooper's Charter is necessary (*The Times*, 10 June 2013, Episode 1). This is similarly connected to notions of more transparent oversight. Overall, the discourse in the quality right-leaning press tended to suggest that mass surveillance may be crucial for our safety but is only justifiable when 'subject to a system of checks and balances in which everybody can have faith' (*The Times*, 11 June 2013, Episode 1). One *Telegraph* commentator suggested:

> *One solution would be for GCHQ to follow the other security agencies in letting in a chink of sunlight: as with MI5 and MI6, explaining more of what it does would not limit its capabilities.* (*Daily Telegraph*, 11 June 2013, Episode 1)

Belief in the positive effects of transparency here seems to be based on the idea that 'sunlight is said to be the best disinfectant' (Brandeis, 1914: 92). Reflecting a more explicit concern with the exercise of state power, several commentators in the left-leaning press put forward the idea that without transparency and accountability, we would be at risk of falling into totalitarianism (e.g. *Guardian*, 25 October 2013, Episode 2b). One commentator/comedian known for his left-wing views (Mark Steel), turned the surveillance and oversight argument on its head, arguing that it should be the governments that are surveilled by the public.

> *So it seems quite reasonable to propose a deal in which the taps on Mrs Merkel's phones stay in place, and all the spying equipment in the world is kept going – it's just the people doing it that's changed. Maybe Edward Snowden can be put in charge. He seems to know how it works.* (*Independent*, 24 October 2013, Episode 2b)

When the revelations first came to light, an initial argument in the left-leaning press was that Obama had broken his earlier promise to confront unrestrained surveillance powers, and 'Obama's NSA' had acted illegally by compelling Verizon to hand over phone records.

> *If the President and Congress would simply obey the Fourth Amendment, this revelation that the government is now spying on citizens' phone data en masse would never have happened. (Guardian, 7 June 2013, Episode 1)*

Accountability became a more dominant theme in discussions over spying on embassies and world leaders (Episode 2). The media discussions were not explicitly related to snooping on world leaders, however, but rather more generally to the role of state power and agencies in attacking civil liberties.

> *It's a democratic necessity that the Snowden leaks are used to bring some genuine accountability to the NSA-GCHQ machine and its lawless industrial-scale espionage. (Guardian, 23 October 2013, Episode 2b)*

Western intelligence services were framed as 'instruments of global dominance' (Guardian, 23 October 2013, Episode 2b), which have an explicit impact on civil liberties. In this argument the issue is not about the balance between security and privacy, but rather about the actions of the political elite and agencies in a global context.

> *What matters is knowing what is being done to protect our freedom so we can judge for ourselves and hold our politicians to account. Without accountability, the state becomes all-powerful and we slip from democracy to dictatorship. Governments have a duty to look after our safety, but in a free and open democracy they also have a duty to look after our liberty. (Guardian, 25 October 2013, Episode 2b)*

One *Guardian* article made the point that, because democratic institutions have failed to hold the intelligence agencies to account, we have to rely on whistle-blowers for the truth (*Guardian*, 11 June 2013, Episode 1). Lack of oversight, transparency, and accountability were also used as central frames in the context of the detention of David Miranda (Episode 3) across all publications. Here, it was the lack of oversight of the use of Schedule 7 – granting authorities the power to stop, search, and hold individuals at ports, airports, and international railway stations – which was brought into question. But again, the *existence* of Schedule 7 was rarely up for debate. Instead, the focus was on the fact that the reasons for holding Miranda for so long under Schedule 7 had not been made clear, and that Schedule 7 needs to be 'radically tightened' to prevent further misuse (*Guardian*, 22 August 2013, Episode 3).

Ultimately, the media's focus on the lack of oversight, transparency, and accountability of the government and security services in the coverage of the episodes following the revelations deflects attention away from the key issues of privacy and security that Snowden hoped to raise. There is an underlying sentiment that, as long as the public is fully informed and appropriate checks and balances are in place, then the use of mass surveillance is justifiable in terms of national security. By cloaking the key issues of privacy and security in calls for greater transparency, oversight and accountability, commentators avoid having to make a stand on either side of the debate, and contribute to normalising practices of surveillance, situating them firmly outside the 'sphere of legitimate controversy' (Hallin, 1986). This reflects an emerging discursive regime which justifies surveillance, as long as it is done openly.

What is also interesting here is that the discourse of transparency was far more prominent in opinionated journalism than in hard news coverage. Data from a larger quantitative content analysis of newspaper coverage (including both 'hard news' and opinionated journalism), with a sample of 538 articles across the same case studies (Wahl-Jorgensen et al., 2015), shows an interesting pattern. When we look at opinions expressed by news sources – a category completely dominated by politicians and other official government voices, which accounted for more than 40% (911 of 2,234 sources coded), there is a clear emphasis on the justification of surveillance. Here, the most frequent opinion was that surveillance should be *increased* or is acceptable and necessary (11.1%). This was followed by the view that the leaks have compromised the work of the intelligence services (7.8%). Arguments that surveillance should be reduced or is unacceptable (7.1%), and that surveillance should be more transparent, while still prominent (4%), appeared less frequently. This dominant discourse understands surveillance as a valuable activity in the interest of national security and one for which both intelligence services and businesses have a responsibility – rather than as primarily problematic for citizens. In opinionated journalism, the view that surveillance is justified in the interest of national security represented the second-most prominent discourse.

Justifying surveillance in the interest of national security

Bolstering the new discursive settlement in aid of the normalisation of surveillance, this discourse did not arise in a vacuum. Rather, there is evidence to suggest a longer standing discursive framing of state interventions that limit civil liberties through a reference to concerns about state security. Along those lines, legislative strategies limiting civil liberties through surveillance have typically been framed as counter-terrorism laws in both government and media discourses (MacDonald and Hunter, 2013; MacDonald et al., 2013). As Picard has argued, there is a long-standing consensus in political theory that, when the existence of the state is threatened, 'ordinary morality' no longer applies (Picard, 2015: 37). In other words, the idea of national security constitutes a discursive trump card overriding any other claims to justice (see also Schulze, 2015).

In the UK context, arguments that justify the restriction of civil liberties have increased in both prevalence and significance since the 7/7 attacks in London. As Clare Birchall has argued, discourses of security and transparency are essential to contemporary practices of governmentality: 'That is to say, states commonly appeal to security as a justification for covert operations and surveillance and offer forms of transparency, or open government, as a form of compensation' (Birchall, 2016: 152). Along those lines, the key forms of justification emerging after the NSA leaks cannot be viewed in isolation, but should rather be seen as emerging from a particular historical context, and coalescing into a set of distinctive arguments. These arguments are premised on the deeply embedded nature of surveillance in our everyday lives (Ganesh, 2016: 167) and the resulting normalisation of 'the watched world' (Lyon, 2007: 11; see also Mathiesen, 2012). At the same time, they dramatise the particularly polarised nature of the media in the UK.

This discourse came across in one quarter of the opinion pieces (20 out of 80) with a particularly strong presence in coverage that came in the wake of the initial leaks (Episode 1; 12 articles). Mass surveillance was framed as crucial to protect the country (national security) and its citizens (individual security) from terrorist attacks. This discourse was largely articulated in the right-leaning press (15 out of the 20 articles), demonstrating that the justification of surveillance is shaped by the polarisation of the British news media. For example, opinion pieces

65

in the quality newspaper the *Daily Telegraph* and tabloid the *Sun* both described bulk data gathering as 'comforting' in the light of security threats:

> *That the NSA and GCHQ should share such information ought to be a cause of comfort rather than concern. They don't gather information for the sake of it – they do it to keep us safer. (Daily Telegraph, 8 June 2013, Episode 1)*

> *[B]ut I feel comforted, not threatened, by the thought that shadowy people are sifting through data to thwart any potential security threats. (Sun, 12 June 2013, Episode 1)*

Some even argued that the state does not have *enough* surveillance powers to keep us safe (*Daily Telegraph*, Episode 1) and the public should trust the state to do what is necessary to prevent security threats.

> *Rather, we should worry that our governments are prevented from snooping enough on the right people. Or doing anything else about them. (Daily Telegraph, 8 June 2013, Episode 1)*

The emphasis on national security as the foremost concern – and surveillance as a necessary response to threats – was often connected with the 'nothing to hide, nothing to fear' argument, particularly in the right-leaning tabloid press.

> *If it's a simple case of the emails and phone calls of ordinary, law-abiding people with nothing to fear being monitored as part of a wider effort to catch terrorist sleeper cell activities before anyone gets hurt, then so what? (Sun, 12 June 2013, Episode 1)*

The 'nothing to fear' discourse is not a distinctively British one, but rather represents a globalised discursive regime that contributes to the justification of surveillance in a variety of contexts. It represents a common-sense articulation of the idea that being under constant surveillance is not only a fact of life in contemporary societies, but also entirely acceptable given the constant terrorist threat. This discourse has taken root in the context of an emerging 'control society' where users 'remain relatively unconcerned with surveillance, accepting the trade-off of greater usability for decreased control' (Best, 2010: 5). Further, it flips arguments in favour of transparency of surveillance practices on their head, suggesting instead that the transparency of individual actions is secured through constant surveillance. It ultimately minimises concerns about privacy and individual rights, highlighting instead the value of 'law-abiding' citizens enabling and accepting regimes of monitoring and surveillance.

Conclusion

The complex discourses at work in the British coverage of the NSA leaks remind us that, not only do particular geographical (and historical) contexts generate their own justifications, but that these are also complicated by the heteronymy of the journalistic field. In this case, coverage of Snowden's revelation became a battleground for arguments that were not merely about trade-offs between security and civil liberties, but also about the role of journalism as it interplays with national and global political forces. In particular, because of the politically polarised nature of the press in Britain, coupled with the central role of the *Guardian* in facilitating the NSA leaks, the discourses in British opinionated journalism were informed by a meta-discourse regarding the boundaries of journalism, the *Guardian* was criticised by right-leaning newspapers for violating its responsibilities to the state by risking national security.

As we have argued, this discursive framing constructs a set of normative assumptions about the boundaries of journalism which suggest that (a) media organisations should avoid the role of political actors in their own right, while (b) remaining committed to patriotic duties in the service of national security. The ideological fault lines of the British press shaped the distinctive ways in which discourses around surveillance were articulated. Nonetheless, a new discursive settlement seems to have emerged, through which acts of mass surveillance remain outside the sphere of legitimate controversy. Instead, surveillance is justified on the basis of national security, provided that this surveillance is carried out in a transparent and accountable manner. And although debates over surveillance are frequently framed with reference to broader global and transnational contexts, the debate remains firmly refracted through the lens of the British political landscape and fought on a long-standing battleground of newspaper partisanship.

It is, then, an interesting example of a particular form of domestication (Clausen, 2004) of global debates, which demonstrates how competition between media organisations has tangible consequences for what kinds of arguments are available to national publics. Mediated debates ultimately unfold within a context where national security is viewed as an indisputable trump card that cannot be questioned or contested.

Note

1 The *Independent* ceased to be printed and went online only in March 2016.

4

News Flashpoints: The Snowden Revelations in the United States[1]

Adrienne Russell and Silvio Waisbord

By now, the events that triggered the coverage of the Snowden revelations are widely known. In June 2013, the *Guardian, New York Times,* and other news organisations reported on massive secret surveillance of citizens and foreign governments conducted by the US government with the complicity of telecommunications companies that granted access to the National Security Agency (NSA). On 5 June, the *Guardian's* first story on the case was published, disclosing that the US Foreign Intelligence Surveillance Court forced Verizon through a secret order to provide access to the NSA to phone records of millions of Americans. On 6 June, a story in the *Washington Post* revealed that the NSA collected digital information from major companies through a programme code-named PRISM. The revelations laid bare unprecedented official invasions of privacy, and generated waves of diplomatic furore as embarrassing details about US and UK spying on international allies became public. Press disclosures were based on information leaked by Edward Snowden who, as an employee of Booz, Allen & Hamilton, worked as contractor for the NSA.

The Snowden revelations not only shed light on the US government's massive covert surveillance operations; they also inspired a rich discursive landscape, as reflected in various journalistic and public responses in the US. They altered journalism, too, by exposing threats to reporting, prompting journalists to learn how to protect sources in the digital era (Lee, 2013), and insisting on the limits of unrealistic attempts at reporter neutrality.[2] Since the initial leaks, there has been a steady rise in the development and use of encryption tools (*Wired*, 16 May 2014). The leaks also seem to have prompted members of the public to reflect on the possible threat to their own freedoms (Preibusch, 2015). Sales of Orwell's classic dystopian novel *1984* skyrocketed soon after the revelations came out (*CNN Money*, 12 June 2013). The leaks set Twitter abuzz with commentary on Snowden's actions, debates about whether he was hero or traitor, and later discussion of the nuances of the leaks (Qin, 2015).

This chapter explores the nature of surveillance discourse in the US news environment, identifying peaks in coverage and documenting key events, people, and themes that shaped stories of the Snowden revelations across legacy and alternative media, to identify and explore the news events that anchored the development of the story. In addition, we introduce the concept of *news flashpoints* as a way of thinking through when peaks in coverage and interest synch up across various types of news media and platforms and across professional–amateur–special interest borders. Our aim is to explore the following key questions. How has the consolidation of a hybrid media system influenced the dynamics of the event in the US context? How are stories sustained and broadened in this new information space? What are the implications for the public in terms of the spectrum of information, interpretations, and points of views made available via this hybrid environment?

Boundaries, hybridity, and flashpoints

Addressing these questions is key to understanding the dynamics of news production in today's networked media environment. Digital networks help facilitate a hybrid environment that features constantly interweaving digital media practices and traditional media practices, products, and technologies. As Andrew Chadwick puts it, blurred boundaries between information and affect, news and entertainment, are part of a media environment marked by 'subtle but important shifts in the balance of power' that shape news production (Chadwick, 2013: 6). Porous boundaries between older and newer media sometimes create a blending of the two and other times create struggle by various actors and institutions in the expanded field as actors seek to maintain and defend particular internal practices. Thomas Gieryn (1983) calls this *boundary work*, or 'the rhetorical and material delimitations of insiders and outsiders, of what counts as ethical practice, and so on'. These are questions ultimately concerning who has the power to control the practices and normative functions of a profession (Lewis, 2012: 2). In the current news environment, as boundaries shift, new practices are adopted, some of which challenge existing journalistic practice and corresponding notions of what journalism ought to do. Some changes extend and bolster the existing functions of legacy journalism, for example watchdogging, truth-telling, and giving-voice-to-the-powerless.

Writing about journalism, Seth Lewis (2015: 220) suggests that what we are witnessing is 'not so much the wholesale collapse of legacy borders, but rather a series of disruptions, all varying in scope and source, coalescing into one vast and complicated terrain of contestation'. So-called boundary work highlights ways power is being negotiated by the media-makers working the borders and going through what Zizi Papacharissi (2015: 6) describes as 'a transitional, but essential stage in finding one's own place in the story'. Papacharissi documents ways people use digital and networked technologies to plug in and contribute to political events. Members of what she terms 'affective publics' participate in social media versions of events, sometimes creating related but separate events, and often using emotion as a way of knowing and sharing in the larger story.

The coverage of the Snowden revelations is a rich site to explore the dynamics between legacy news outlets and emerging forms of journalism in order to better understand the circumstances in which discourse becomes dynamic and varied through the mingling of different news actors. The then *Guardian* editor Alan Rusbridger (2015) lamented what he sees as the simplistic public debate that has grown out of the Snowden revelations and pointed out that 'there are multiple public interests' related to the story but that the press tends to cover only privacy and security. He was referencing the UK press but the same rings true in the US, where discussion of the issues surrounding the leaks has been fairly narrow. Yet, at the same time, and sometimes only outside traditional news outlets, there is an expanding set of issues being discussed and reported. Building on the notion of journalistic hybridity and contested boundaries, we introduce the concept of *news flashpoints* as a heuristic for making sense of the ways new genres and actors can help create a more robust and varied discourse, expanding the sphere of legitimate debate and the set of possible interpretations and understandings of news events.

Research design

In exploring how the story played out among US news outlets, we analyse frequency of coverage and range of themes presented in stories triggered by the Snowden revelations between June 2013 and June 2014. We examine coverage produced for multiple news outlets, in various genres and from across the ideological spectrum.

Our sample includes two 'first-tier' professional mainstream newspapers, the *New York Times* and the *Wall Street Journal*, and several 'second-tier' news outlets with a distinct and influential voice: *Mother Jones* (a left-of-centre news magazine), the *National Review* (a right-of-centre magazine), *Electronic Frontier Foundation* (EFF, a non-profit online civil liberties advocacy group), and the *Verge* (a tech-focused news outlet). The notion of first- and second-tier news was developed by Orville Schell in reference to the US media environment in 2004, analysing coverage of the onset of the 2003 Iraq War. He wrote: 'The lower tier populated by niche publications, alternative media outlets, Public Broadcasting Service, National Public Radio, and internet sites, host[ed] the broadest spectrum of viewpoints. The upper tier populated by the major broadcast outlets, newspapers, and magazines, allow[ed] a much more limited bandwidth of opinion' (Schell, 2004: p. v). Tier one, then, includes corporate-owned media that by and large adhere to traditional practices of reporting. They tend to privilege authoritative sources and traditional notions of objectivity that limit the 'bandwidth of opinion', or points of view that fall outside the status quo, as Schell puts it. We included these particular outlets in our sample because they represent various news genres as well as ideological and topical areas of emphasis. Left-wing and right-wing publications of smaller distribution (*Mother Jones* and the *National Review*) as well as outlets focused primarily on the legal and technological aspects of the story (EFF and the *Verge* respectively) were considered within our sample to account for both the possibility of a wider range of arguments and the expanded genres and news styles.

In the *New York Times*, the story received the most attention in the first month after the initial leaks (119 stories in June), and then progressively dwindled (to 56 in July, 34 in August, and 27 in September 2013). It picked up interest again in October (52 stories), and remained in the headlines frequently until the end of the year (43 stories in November, 48 in December). From January to July of 2014, the amount of coverage fell off significantly.

Then we compared the *New York Times* peaks to peaks in the other outlets in our sample.[3] We found that each outlet's coverage conformed to a similar series of peaks over the year studied. To track public interest levels, we looked at Google search trends for the term 'NSA' in the

United States, as Google Trends reveals how often this search term is entered relative to the total search-volume across selected regions of the world.[4]

Flashpoints

Flashpoints are news events with enormous bursts of attention driven by legacy, alternative, and social media. Taken together, the coverage during these flashpoints raised and addressed a series of specific questions related to the revelations. Did secret NSA surveillance produce information that prevented terrorist attacks? How transparent should the programme be? Can information considered of national interest be obtained without violating the rights of American citizens? Should private companies comply with government plans to monitor citizen communication? Who owns information and/or decides the limits between private and public interest? What is the correct interpretation of the First Amendment on these matters? And what role should a journalist and news outlet take in reporting on the story and advocating government transparency?

Answers to these questions and the treatment of the key themes that drove coverage of the Snowden revelations varied according to the editorial standpoint or specialised focus and type of news outlet. What follows is an analysis of each flashpoint, which includes an outline of key events and circumstances that drove it and an overview of the different themes and approaches produced by various outlets in our sample. We identified five flashpoints determined by a synchronised intensity of coverage and increased frequency of related Google searches and illustrated by the uniformity of peaks. Although the story was consistently covered, the overall volume of news stories progressively declined during the year studied.

Flashpoint one: 6–19 June 2013

During the first flashpoint, 6–19 June 2013, three types of events sustained the story: informational events, including Snowden's strategically placed leaks to the press; actual events, including details of his background and cross-continental movements; and official events, Obama and other government and technology industry leaders commenting or acting in response to the leaks.

On 5 June, the *Guardian* published leaks that revealed a secret court order requiring Verizon, one of the largest telecom companies in the US, to turn over the phone records of millions of Americans to the US government. And on 6 June, a second story revealed the previously undisclosed PRISM programme, which gives the NSA direct access to data held by Google, Facebook, Apple, and other US internet giants. The technology companies involved all denied that they had set up 'backdoor access' to their systems for the US government. These two initial leaks launched the first and most coverage-intensive flashpoint.

During this flashpoint, Snowden's actions propelled the story forward, as did his proximity to reporters and news organisations. Journalists played critical roles in the launch and the nature of the story, acting as both the sources and producers of coverage. Snowden's strategy to leak the story to selected top global news organisations ensured wide dissemination and intense attention during the first weeks. This included the original story on 6 June and Snowden's introduction to the public in an interview with the *Guardian*, posted on YouTube and other video-sharing platforms, that was widely circulated and covered across media outlets around the world. The staggered sequence of leaks in major global publications sustained the story for several weeks across the world.

The journalists at the heart of the leaks too were scattered around the globe: Barton Gellman in Washington DC, Glenn Greenwald in Rio, Laura Poitras in Berlin, Alan Rusbridger in London. This was by design, as Rusbridger explains it: '[Snowden] picked a number of people in different geographies ... That made it a complicated story for the National Security Agency to deal with, in large part because it would be difficult to use conventional ways to stop Glenn in Rio from publishing' (Rusbridger, 2015). Indeed, Snowden carefully planned what and how the leaks should be introduced to maximise journalistic and public attention. The relations he established with journalists, his familiarity with the documents and his insight concerning how to introduce them to the public, and his own intrigue as a now-public figure helped ensure that the story had legs.

The press was an essential part of Snowden's plan from the beginning and after the launch of the story he ceded control of the leaked documents, as well as the news about them, to Greenwald and the other journalists to whom he handed over the files. At that point the story came to depend on the workflow of journalists. Rusbridger explains:

[What was published when] was determined really by how long it took to go through the documents. [After Hong Kong] everything slowed down because it was much more complicated. We didn't have Snowden sitting there saying 'I can guide you here.' We had these documents here and had no idea what they meant. We had to work it out ourselves. (Rusbridger, 2015)

With only six *Guardian* journalists combing through the material at any given time, the process was slow.

In June 2013, both the *New York Times* and the *Wall Street Journal* repeatedly addressed the legality and constitutionality of the programme; the effectiveness of the programme in curtailing terrorist attacks; and the issues of privacy, oversight, and transparency or lack thereof. While the former ran several op-eds criticising the NSA,[5] nearly every related opinion piece and column in the latter argued that US national security depends on government surveillance, and that Snowden put Americans in danger by betraying 'national secrets'.[6] Several pointed to legal precedent in which the US Supreme Court interpreted the Constitution to allow for what one could call mass surveillance.

The *National Review* and *Mother Jones*, national magazines at opposite poles of the ideological spectrum, echoed the points of view and themes of the *Wall Street Journal* and *New York Times* respectively. Their overtly opinionated style, however, allowed for more open critique of political leaders, media reports, and the NSA programmes revealed by Snowden, introducing new themes and a wider range of perspectives to the coverage. The *National Review* repeatedly called for the prosecution of Snowden, criticised journalists for their role in facilitating the leaks, and defended the NSA and what they argued was the constitutionality of the secret programme. Where it diverged from the *Wall Street Journal*, it veered sharply to the right, introducing a range of arguments absent from more mainstream publications – by calling responses to the story an overreaction, for example, or merely a public relations problem (*Wall Street Journal*, 7 June 2015).

In contrast, *Mother Jones* provided a different set of arguments about the broader significance of the revelations. For example, they addressed the fact that under the current set of circumstances in the US, leaks and whistle-blowers are 'our only means of obtaining information about government activities', thus pointing out that increasing government opacity corresponds to increased demands for citizen transparency

(*Mother Jones*, 17 June 2013). *Mother Jones* also provided more nuanced analysis of the issues surrounding notions of privacy, surveillance, and government/citizen relations, cutting through the technicalities of the legal arguments and publishing corrections and explainers in response to official statements and media reports. These opinion magazines offer a distinct and influential voice and introduce an expanded set of arguments and points of view around the key themes of the story. They therefore expand beyond the newspapers' focus on privacy and surveillance, albeit from ideological points of view that mirror those reflected opposing realms of the political establishment.

EFF and the *Verge* offered more nuanced treatment of the technological and legal issues related to the story as well as salient critiques of both media coverage and the treatment of the revelations by politicians. These outlets also produced coverage that was more expansive than the coverage produced by the newspaper and magazine outlets examined so far. Beginning on 5 June, on their 'NSA Primary Sources' page, for example, EFF curated all direct coverage of the leaks from *Der Spiegel*, the *Guardian,* and the *Washington Post* as well as coverage of leaks from lesser-known publications such as the *Intercept.*[7] In this way, EFF set itself up as a repository of information for journalists, lawyers, researchers, and members of the public who wanted to keep tabs on the story or build on this background to produce reports of their own. The EFF archive also focused heavily on coverage of legal and industry happenings related to the leaks. For example, the outlet highlighted what various social media platforms were doing to step up protections for users and recorded the various legal cases being brought against the NSA, many of which were brought by EFF itself. EFF also frequently ran pieces aimed at providing readers with information on how to fight back and protect themselves from surveillance, which positioned the EFF not only as the go-to source for primary documents and initial reporting but also as an advocate site focused on helping publics and journalists protect themselves against the NSA spying.[8]

Flashpoint two: 25 July to 24 August 2013

The second flashpoint, 25 July to 24 August, was driven in part by Snowden's movements during his quest for asylum, which provided a series of news pegs that carried the story forward. On 24 July, the day before the onset of this flashpoint, a lawyer advising Snowden announced that Snowden would stay at the Moscow Airport until his asylum status was resolved. Images and testimonies from Snowden's arrival in Russia galvanised press and public attention.

Along with Snowden's location and status, a continuous flow of leaks and official responses to those leaks drove coverage during this peak period. On 31 July, the US Senate Judiciary Committee held a hearing on oversight of FISA (Foreign Intelligence Surveillance Act), the US federal law that prescribes procedures for electronic and physical surveillance, which has been repeatedly amended since the 9/11 attacks in the US. This hearing was followed on 9 August by the White House release of a legal justification for the programmes, claiming the bulk collection of telephone metadata was legal under the Patriot Act (Section 215), while positing a new, expanded definition of the word 'relevance'. The other major event during this peak period came with the 1 August publication of a *Guardian* story that revealed the US had been secretly funding the United Kingdom's Government Communication Headquarters (GCHQ).[9] By this point, a pattern had been established in how the Snowden–NSA story was being covered: major leaks by a leading global news organisation were followed by news about official and industry responses as well as proceedings from congressional and judicial hearings. This pattern continued through the end of 2013.

New York Times opinion pieces in this period dealt largely with President Obama's reaction to the NSA revelations, criticising Obama for failing to follow through with specific, meaningful actions. Two pieces, for example, pointed to the gulf between the President's rhetoric and his policy (*New York Times*, 31 July 2013, 9 August 2013). Following the initial peak period pattern, the *National Review* defended the NSA, turning its focus after the first month away from Snowden towards both the legal justification for the secret programmes and towards criticism of Obama and the NSA's failure to better explain the effectiveness of the programme and the protections in place to guard against civil rights abuses (*National Review*, 22 August 2013). *Mother Jones* provided analysis of the issues surrounding notions of privacy, surveillance, and government/citizen relations. EFF focused on reporting on law and the tech industry, and ran several pieces aimed at providing readers with info on how to fight back against the government programmes and protect themselves from snooping. Contrasting significantly with the content of other outlets, the *Verge* focused on technology-related issues. It reported, for example, on other publications' information about XKeyscore and NSA's ability to remotely activate laptop mics (*Verge*, 31 July 2013) and on the creation of an NSA Tumblr blog (*Verge*, 21 August 2013). Some of these stories were first covered in other media and linked to from the *Verge*. Even when the site did not break the story, or first raise the issue, the *Verge* drew from diverse sources and focused on niche topics, carving out a unique area of coverage.

Flashpoint three: 24 October to 13 November 2013

The 24 October to 13 November flashpoint was driven by several major stories, including two US government hearings on the programme (the House Intelligence Committee hearing on 29 October and the Senate Judiciary Committee hearing on transparency 13 November), and a *Washington Post* exposé on NSA hacking into Google and Yahoo data centres (*Washington Post*, 30 October 2013). During this flashpoint, NSA spying on international leaders was also revealed, which prompted extensive discussion of the differences between domestic and international surveillance.

Brewing since the initial leaks, debate about the role of journalism intensified during this period. This happened especially after the now-famous 27 October 2013 exchange between *New York Times* Executive Editor Bill Keller and Glenn Greenwald, bringing debates about journalism solidly into the centre of the story. In a *New York Times* column titled, 'Is Glenn Greenwald the future of news?' Keller refers to Greenwald not as a journalist but a 'blogger' and then goes on to write: 'I find much to admire in America's history of crusading journalists, from the pamphleteers to the muckrakers to the New Journalism of the 1960s to the best of today's activist bloggers.' Whether or not the terms 'crusader' and 'blogger' were meant in the pejorative when used by high-ranking journalists like Keller, the internet lit up in defence of Greenwald's work. Greenwald, too, articulated the tension between his practice and the practices of Keller and many other members of the journalism establishment. After acknowledging the excellent reporting done by establishment media venues over the last few decades, Greenwald wrote:

> I don't think anyone contends that what has become (rather recently) the standard model for a reporter – concealing one's subjective perspectives or what appears to be 'opinions' – precludes good journalism.
>
> But this model has also produced lots of atrocious journalism and some toxic habits that are weakening the profession. A journalist who is

petrified of appearing to express any opinions will often steer clear of declarative sentences about what is true, opting instead for a cowardly and unhelpful 'here's-what-both-sides-say-and-I-won't-resolve-the-conflicts' formulation. That rewards dishonesty on the part of political and corporate officials who know they can rely on 'objective' reporters to amplify their falsehoods without challenge (i.e., reporting is reduced to 'X says Y' rather than 'X says Y and that's false'). (Greenwald in Keller, 2013)

Even beyond the high-profile and widely circulated debate, journalists became major actors in the story. News organisations frequently cited and linked to one another, reporting, critiquing, and expanding on each other's coverage. Even the *Wall Street Journal*, which rarely links beyond its own pages, reported on stories by the *Guardian, Washington Post,* and other outlets that originally published the leaks. In turn, journalism itself became a subject of controversy. Intelligence and security actors condemned the press for assisting Snowden and for collaborating in activities that they believed endangered US interests and safety. Others applauded the decision of news organisations to help bring Snowden's revelations to the public.

Meanwhile, the *Wall Street Journal* kept up its defence of the NSA, dismissing the notion that US spying violated domestic laws or international norms. One editorial cited former French Foreign Minister Bernard Kouchner as saying: 'Everyone is listening to everyone else. But we don't have the same means as the US, which makes us jealous' (*Wall Street Journal,* 29 October 2013). *Mother Jones* continued to challenge the programmes, including in one how-to article headlined 'How to Keep the NSA Out of Your Computer' (*Mother Jones,* September/October 2013).

In addition to coverage of NSA-related legal action, EFF ran several pieces critiquing media coverage. One led with the headline 'EFF to *New York Times*: Don't Get Fooled Again by Claims of NSA Spying "Legality"' (EFF, 11 November 2013). The organisation's outlet also ran a story about how it was representing ProPublica in an effort to bring secret court opinions to light (EFF, 12 November 2013). During this period the *Verge* tracked the ongoing revelations about the relationship between the NSA and industry, typically by highlighting key coverage published by the *Washington Post* and other publications. The *Verge* also ran a more investigative article concerning global internet privacy regulation and the possible future Balkanisation of the infrastructure of the internet given international concerns about US spying (EFF, 8 November 2013).

Flashpoint four: 12 December to 10 January 2013

The final flashpoint of 2013, from 12 December to 10 January 2014, also largely involved coverage of official responses and more NSA document leaks. On 16 December, US Federal Judge Richard Leon ruled NSA mass phone surveillance likely unconstitutional, and on 18 December a review group directed by Obama released a report. There was also continued flow of reporting during this period, most notably coverage of a *Der Spiegel* piece on an internal NSA document that revealed spying tools used by the agency.

One recurring argument in the pages of the *Wall Street Journal* and *New York Times* during this flashpoint was that it is 'human nature' to abuse power or snoop and therefore protections against such abuses must be bolstered through legislation.[10] This argument sometimes adopted technologically determinist tones. A *New York Times* column argued that 'These technological toys turn everyone into thieves' (17 December 2013). The implicit suggestion seems to be that we are dealing with fundamental questions about the protection of citizens' rights in governments; these questions have not come up in the past only because they were 'invisible' by virtue of circumstance and available technology.

Closely related is an increased concentration of editorial interest in governmental checks and balances. Similarly, and directly driven by interest in Judge Leon's December ruling on the likely unconstitutionality of NSA activities, came a recurring distinction among written law, interpretation of law, and sometimes the 'spirit of the law'. The *New York Times* cited violation of the Fourth Amendment as justification for the illegality of the spying programmes (*New York Times*, 18 December 2013) and by contrast, the *Wall Street Journal* cited *Smith v. Maryland* (18 December 2013)[11] frequently, suggesting that it should be up to elected officials to determine the law rather than the courts. The debate essentially is represented across media as a contest between judicial and executive powers; that is, whether the courts or politicians should decide the issue.

Mother Jones and the *Verge* cut through the technicalities of the legal arguments and published corrections and explainers. For example, *Mother Jones* ran a story with the headline '10 Myths About NSA Surveillance

That Need Debunking' (*Mother Jones*, 10 January 2014), and the *Verge* ran another media criticism piece headlined 'Don't Be Fooled By the *60 Minutes* Report on the NSA' (*Verge*, 15 December 2013). Unlike most other media, the *Verge* ran little coverage of federal court cases and instead provided in-depth coverage of the technical aspects of the revelations. These included an item on the tech industry meeting with Obama (17 December 2013), one on Apple's denial that they knew iPhones were hacked (31 December 2013), and one on the lack of anonymity of metadata (26 December 2013) among other more tech- and industry-focused stories.

Flashpoint five: 16–28 January 2014

During the 16–28 January flashpoint, key news events included the *Guardian* revelations that the NSA was collecting text messages, Obama's 17 January speech on the NSA, and a continued flow of leaks. At this point, six months into the story, coverage became more nuanced, with the most prominent recurring feature being an emphasis on the need to rethink both rights and laws in response to new technology and a changing society. The notions of Constitutional rights and precedents arose in these discussions as starting points to be examined and interrogated rather than as firm guides for reform.

In his 17 January speech, Obama defended the NSA and outlined a series of reforms but stopped short of demanding an end to the bulk collection of American citizens' phone data. The *Wall Street Journal* emphasised the technology and phone companies' responses to the speech and the joint statement by a group of tech companies including Google, Microsoft, and Facebook that they would continue to work with government to sort out the still 'unresolved issues'. One *National Review* article outlined the 'collective "whew"' of conservatives that 'Obama did not give in to the pleas of the anti-war Left and cripple the NSA completely, or end the collection and analysis of telephone metadata'. The article also criticised him for 'praising Snowden as some kind of hero, instead of the traitor that he is' (*National Review*, 17 January 2014). Other coverage, including in the *New York Times*, criticised Obama on several counts: for his failure to acknowledge Snowden's role in pushing for reform; for failing to address the mass collection of data in the first place; and for skirting questions about whether or not the programmes had been effective in thwarting terrorist attacks (*New York Times*, 17 January 2014). EFF put out a report 'Rating Obama's NSA Reform Plan: EFF Scorecard Explained', on how the President's announcements stack up against what they called '12 common sense fixes that should be a minimum for reforming NSA surveillance' (EFF, 17 January 2014). The *Verge* ran several articles on Obama's policy statements and their reception by political and cultural leaders, including one on coverage of a Jon Stewart bit mocking Obama's response (*Verge*, 21 January 2014). Other articles demonstrate the opinions expressed by other leaders and analysts. Take, for example, an open letter the outlet ran from cryptologists stating their opposition to mass surveillance (*Verge*, 26 January 2013).

Across all of the flashpoints, there is clearly thematic complexity and distinct areas of focus among the outlets – some acting as repositories and consumer advocates (EFF) and others reflecting the viewpoints of the domestic political elite (the *New York Times* and *Wall Street Journal*). This made for diverse coverage that addressed a wide range of issues and perspectives.

Even so, we see coverage that is heavily focused on the US political elite. Contrary to recent research that suggests news stories linked to geopolitics are becoming not 'solely domestic or foreign news' (Berglez, 2008), but instead circulate within, and help foster, a broader, global public sphere (Volkmer, 2014), the Snowden revelation news flashpoints were overwhelmingly connected to US-specific actors, events, and legal and political contexts. This occurred despite the fact that global actors and news organisations played a central role in the evolution of the story from the beginning. The *Wall Street Journal* and *New York Times* relied heavily on elite US sources, namely public officials and corporate leaders, who dominated coverage of the revelations, mirroring the political discourse that treated privacy and security as the main topics of public interest, downplaying some of the more nuanced questions we see addressed in other outlets. This US focus was reflected in the other outlets in the US sample. Across all publications, for example, columnists were more likely to debate whether the NSA's extensive surveillance was constitutional or unconstitutional than the more universal questions of whether it was moral or immoral. Similarly, the near-constant debates about whether Snowden was a hero or a villain was always focused on the perceived risks or benefits the leaks posed for the US. There was little concern beyond US interests. The domestic lens still would appear prominent and fogged over with nationalism.

The predominance of both domestic and official angles is underscored by the fact of what was not covered extensively. Several significant international stories fell outside flashpoints, such as when British MPs forced the *Guardian* to destroy its servers, when Greenwald's partner David Miranda was detained at Heathrow, and when the story broke that the NSA was spying on foreign agencies. Each of these stories was reported by *Der Spiegel* on 30 June 2013, which was outside any of the flashpoints. There were also no flashpoints in coverage around nationwide protests in the US, such as the 'Restore the Fourth' rallies that took place across the US on 4 July protesting NSA spying or 'The Day We Fight Back' protests on 11 February 2014. This suggests that perhaps what is considered newsworthy still depends in large part on newsrooms and their elite sources.

Flashpoints as a heuristic

Through this examination of flashpoint coverage, and the events and thematic complexity that shaped them, we can trace the anatomy of a flashpoint as connected to events and actors that are traditionally considered newsworthy but also sustained and expanded by the hybrid context of the news media environment. To elaborate on this point, we consider news flashpoints as a heuristic that helps us think through a new communication phenomenon grounded in the dynamics of changing and diversified news landscapes. In the case of the opinionated debate of the Snowden revelations over the one-year period we studied (2013–14), flashpoints connected to traditional newsworthy events or statements by key actors both propelled the debate but also expanded the themes and storylines included in the coverage. By doing so, these attention moments broadened the possible interpretations of the ongoing story beyond simplistic debates focused on a conception of public interest limited only to privacy and security.

Flashpoints can be considered examples of Gaye Tuchman's (1973) 'what a story' category: meaningful, unexpected, unusual events that capture enormous attention from newsrooms and deviate from routine news production. Like the 'what a story' events, news flashpoints are focused on remarkable occurrences that draw wide attention from newsrooms and publics. Yet because multiple actors are engaged in disseminating news and views, 'news flashpoints' are more complex stories than the typical 'what a story'. Whereas the latter are relatively straightforward, displaying consistent narratives largely controlled by legacy outlets, the former are shaped by numerous sources that are not bounded by standard news norms or ideological constraints. News flashpoints reflect hybrid dynamics and new factors shaping their visibility and duration. No doubt, legacy news outlets depart from routinised procedures during news flashpoints just like they do during traditional 'what a story' news. The main difference is that those contributing to news flashpoints monitor and report on a wider set of raw information – the flood of information and opinion, including viral bits, that saturates the hybrid environment after initial revelations are published.

The rush of information around specific subjects clearly overflows the traditional boundaries of news production. Thus, news flashpoints are not simply comprised of content produced by legacy news. They display multiple layers of information with different origins and are activated by news users – posting, commentary, sharing in social media as well as internet searches. Because multiple sources and actors join in, flashpoints lack the kind of neat narrative or temporal development that characterise traditional news stories. They are multi-layered stories around central events. They reflect the rather chaotic convergence of multiple forces producing and sharing news and commentary in today's news ecology. And yet, just as with traditional news, they are event-oriented since they are largely driven by conventional happenings and values that define newsworthiness.

News flashpoints, then, are different from media events (Dayan and Katz, 1992). Like media events, they direct a significant amount of news and public attention to central social, political, and cultural issues. Both produce swells of coverage concentrated on specific events and matters. News flashpoints, however, are far from being organised, well-choreographed events staged by authorities. In fact, they are unpredictable, changing, and unscripted largely because many actors are engaged. Unlike media events, they are not news phenomena manufactured by those in power who exercise relatively tight control over events and developments. Instead, they feature the participation of multiple publics, making them open-ended affairs without a pre-established script. In the networked public sphere (Benkler et al., 2013), various actors are able to shape and sustain news stories. Thus, if the ceremonial and reserved tone of broadcast journalists is typical of news events, a cacophony of scattered and noisy voices dominate news flashpoints. Consequently, news flashpoints are not 'single stories' about a subject: the nation, community, freedom, or other ideological constructions that are typically celebrated by media events. Because they have an open structure, news flashpoints are formed by several layers of narratives that – although focused on the same events – highlight different aspects and meanings.

Indeed, flashpoints are unique to the networked environment, and may at times fulfil what Yochai Benkler calls the networked Fourth Estate, which differs from the traditional press because it includes a diverse set of actors not merely an exclusive group of major news outlets. To Benkler, it is precisely this diversity that makes the internet an effective force in spurring public discussion. He writes:

> The freedom that the internet provides to networked individuals and cooperative associations to speak their minds and organize around their causes has been deployed over the past decade to develop new, networked models of the fourth estate. These models circumvent the social and organizational frameworks of traditional media, which played a large role in framing the balance between freedom and responsibility of the press. (Benkler, 2011: 1)

He sees emerging a new model of watchdogging, 'one that is neither purely networked nor purely traditional but is rather a mutualistic interaction between the two' (2011: 68).

Finally, news flashpoints should not be mistaken for information cascades. Information cascades refer to flows of messages and opinion among the public (Myers and Leskovec, 2014; Neuman et al., 2014; Pei et al., 2015). They are not necessarily triggered or continued by news organisations, but instead are instigated and maintained by various actors. News organisations may play a role, but they are not necessarily central to the dynamics of information cascades. Although both news flashpoints and information cascades refer to the diffusion of information and have similar 'bursty' dynamics in today's networked digital landscape, these conceptualise and highlight different aspects of the current media environment. Cascades generally comprise a wide range of content, including rumours, gossip, news, and data. News flashpoints, in turn, specifically refer to news and information originally triggered by journalistic reporting and determined by the use of conventional journalistic values. News organisations play different roles in news flashpoints and information cascades: whereas they are central to the former by publishing original stories that spark attention to specific issues, they might not necessarily occupy central positions or nodes in the latter. Therefore, the diffusion patterns of news flashpoints are comparatively easier to identify, for they feature in a dominant position news organisations acting in their traditional gatekeeping role. Certainly, flashpoints may initiate and bleed into information cascades, but they are primarily a journalistic phenomenon, attesting to persistent linkages among news outlets.

Conclusion

The idea of news flashpoints is meant to deepen our understanding of the changing dynamics in the hybrid news landscape by distinguishing key moments in which legacy and alternative news outlets create and sustain a burst of attention. Such flashpoints include not only news that is carefully constructed by those in power, but also information cascades that flow from various sources and do not necessarily have connections to journalistic institutions or elite sources. The concept introduces the idea of examining when and how various components/actors of the news landscape come together around coverage of the same events, even though their editorial position and focus may be different. Further work is necessary to refine its heuristic value as well as its explanatory power to understand news dynamics in today's media landscape. This analysis suggests that flashpoints may be particularly good instances to observe the blurring of traditional boundaries and mingling among outlets. Although we chose to look at peaks and themes, flashpoints could also be examined by looking at the circulation of news topics and content in social media, and by documenting the links among various outlets.

Debate on the Snowden revelation in the US outlets examined here demonstrates the enduring influence of elite legacy newspaper outlets. The persistence of the conventional professional practices of Western journalism among key legacy news organisations (Waisbord, 2013) focused attention on explosive revelations involving elite actors, a whistle-blower who worked for a major firm consulting with the US government, prominent officials in the US government, and in US-based internet companies. The outlets also focused on issues central to the ideology of US democracy, including privacy, security, transparency, and freedom. At the same time, these stories resulted in more robust and sustained coverage created through a mingling across genres of news-related media that expanded to meta-coverage in examining the roles, genres, and purpose of journalism itself.

Even though Snowden identifies as a hacker and is likely more versed in the nuances of online information than in the norms of traditional journalism, he saw the press as an essential platform for disclosing the leaks. As he told *Washington Post* reporter Barton Gellman:

> 'For me, in terms of personal satisfaction, the mission's already accomplished ... I already won. As soon as the journalists were able to work, everything that I had been trying to do was validated. Because, remember, I didn't want to change society. I wanted to give society a chance to determine if it should change itself.' Snowden was convinced that the only way to bring up attention and hopefully trigger changes was to ensure front-page news. (*Washington Post*, 23 December 2013)

Looking at coverage through the lens of the concept of flashpoints puts in evidence the consolidation of a multi-layered information ecology of connected new and old platforms. Legacy news organisations retain a prominent position in a crowded, noisy, dispersed, borderless, and ever-expanding networked landscape. The overall information environment, however, is largely different than in the past, as stories are subjected to new, unpredictable dynamics in a crowded and fluid landscape. Stories get shared, commented upon, challenged, and used to advance additional coverage. They engender unpredictable information-sharing sustained by a plethora of traditional and new actors.

In their analysis of the *Guardian*'s role in the coverage of the Snowden–NSA revelations, Chadwick and Collister (2014) point out ways legacy news outlets are reasserting themselves through 'boundary-drawing power', or the ability to leverage resources and established practices to make the best use of the expanded networked environment, essentially by rejecting previous intentional insularity. They describe various logics at work, arguing that, in its reporting on Snowden's leaks, the *Guardian* was able to combine the expertise and resources of commercial media with emerging digital logics.

The fact that there are different practices and processes developing around different contexts calls into question the notion of a singular media logic, a concept that threads through much of the recent scholarship on journalism and political communication. Indeed, the idea of an emergent set of logics around media production and use is brought over from the mass-media era (Altheide and Snow, 1979). This chapter suggests, however, that there is no longer a common set of operating instructions, even within various forms or genres of news media. There are now multiple competing logics, which makes them not 'logics' at all but something more variable and fluid. This can be more usefully thought of as various overlapping and contesting *sensibilities*, or ways of understanding and assessing what is good or valuable in news or in any given genre. The concept of sensibilities gets us away from the idea that there is a codified set of forces dictating how media function (Russell, 2016).

Certainly, at a time when boundaries of journalism are undergoing significant changes and debate (Carlson and Lewis, 2015), legacy news organisations continue to rely on traditional journalistic norms and practices that define newsworthiness and professional ethics in ways that firm up boundaries of expertise in relation to other actors in the field, including other news outlets, bloggers, citizen reporters, sources, and marketers. Even so, while in the case of the Snowden revelations the flashpoints were driven by conventional news factors, coverage from across a broad spectrum of platforms shaped the flashpoint. In fact, the Snowden–NSA 'story' became different stories, focused on multiple themes and interpretative frames.

As outlined above, EFF covered issues of security and online civil liberties and acted as a repository of information. The *Verge* highlighted the technology industry and both tools used to spy and to resist surveillance. Conservative media focused on the implications of the revelation for national security, dismissed concerns about privacy, and condemned Snowden. Progressive media championed Snowden and engaged with issues of privacy and government transparency. Legacy newspapers mostly covered the doings of political and economic elites and at times publicly debated the implications of new forms of reporting put in evidence by the Snowden leaks, as illustrated by the Keller–Greenwald debate. And published leaks became fodder for social media, search engines, and other platforms that afforded their own particular takes on the story and ways of covering it (Klinger and Svensson, 2014; van Dijck and Poell, 2013). Legacy news also became the subject for multiple news outlets imbued with different understandings of news, ideological values, and interests.

During the flashpoints, the enormous volume of information and opinion generated by news organisations lacked a singular logic. Even though a series of stories focused on the same elite actors and actions that first appeared in legacy news organisations, the coverage was not homogeneous. Rather it included multiple stories, angles, forms, meanings, and genres all addressing similar issues: privacy, surveillance, security, and whistle-blowing. News organisations offered different frames and were driven by different sets of practices and values that determined what was important to highlight, investigate, or consider about the story.

Why do news flashpoints matter to understand news and public life? The NSA case was a rare opportunity for journalism in the US and around the world, as this book demonstrates, to give relatively sustained attention to critical and complex issues such as privacy, security, government, and corporate transparency. The Snowden revelations and subsequent events put those issues centre stage, provoking public debate across a range of media platforms. Given that journalism continues to be a central 'sense-making' (Hartley, 2011) institution, providing resources for societies to understand and communicate about public issues, it is important to analyse when, why, and how practices broadly related to journalism yield coverage of issues of public concern over an extended period of time.

Undoubtedly, the overall information ecology in which legacy journalism operates has substantially changed. We should not, however, assume that traditional journalistic values guiding news decisions, and ultimately shaping news flashpoints, have also been transformed or become less important, even as we demonstrate that new media have extended these flashpoints in new and interesting ways. The flashpoints examined here suggest the enduring importance of the traditional press and the significant contribution of an expanded set of news platforms, styles, and actors to the contemporary journalism landscape.

Notes

1 Parts of this chapter also appear in Russell & Waisbord, 2017.
2 Bill Keller, 'Is Glenn Greenwald the future of news?' *New York Times*, 27 Oct. 2013. www.nytimes.com/2013/10/28/opinion/a-conversation-in-lieu-of-a-column.html?pagewanted=all and_r=3 and.
3 Peaks for the *New York Times*, the *Wall Street Journal*, the *Verge* and *Mother Jones* were determined by counting the number of stories that came up using the search NSA and/or Snowden on Lexis Nexis. The *Verge* and EFF were tabulated differently because they are not indexed on Lexis Nexis and are more accurately tallied based on the category tags they are assigned. Articles

tagged with the terms NSA, Privacy or Surveillance were counted; those with more than one term were tallied only once.

4   For more on how the Google Trends tool works see http://insidesearch. blogspot.co.il/2012/09/insights-into-what-world-is-searching.html.

5   See e.g. 'President Obama's Dragnet', 6 June 2013. http://www.nytimes. com/2013/06/07/opinion/president-obamas-dragnet.html. 'Peeping President Obama', 8 June 2013. http://www.nytimes.com/2013/06/09/opinion/sunday/ dowd-peeping-president-obama.html.

6   See e.g. 'Leaking secrets empowers terrorists.' *Wall Street Journal*, 9 June 2013. http://www.wsj.com/articles/SB100014241278873246343045785354924214 80524) and 'Thank you for data-mining.' *Wall Street Journal*, 7 June 2013. http://online.wsj.com/news/articles/SB10001424127887324299104578529373 994191586.

7   NSA Primary Sources page: https://www.eff.org/nsa-spying/nsadocs.

8   See e.g. 'Call now to oppose NSA spying.' EFF, 18 June 2013. 'The NSA word games explained: how the government deceived Congress in the debate over surveillance powers.' EFF, 11 June 2013.

9   FISA is the law under which the NSA should have operated. It authorises the government to conduct surveillance in certain situations without meeting all of the requirements of the Fourth Amendment that apply under criminal law, but requires that an independent Foreign Intelligence Surveillance Court oversee that surveillance to ensure that Americans with no ties to foreign terrorist organisations or other 'foreign powers' are not spied upon. FISA was significantly loosened by the Patriot Act (which, for example, allowed it to be used for some criminal investigations), and parts of it now stand in clear violation of the Constitution's Fourth Amendment in the view of the ACLU and many others. However, even the post-Patriot Act version of FISA does not authorise the President to conduct warrantless eavesdropping on US citizens or permanent legal residents in the US without an order from the FISA Court. It is that very court order requirement, imposed to protect innocent Americans, that the President has ignored.

10 See e.g. 'Virtual reality, real spies.' *New York Times*, 20 Dec. 2013. http://www. nytimes.com/2013/11/09/opinion/why-do-brits-accept-surveillance.html. 'From metal detectors to metadata.' *New York Times*, 22 Dec. 2013. http:// online.wsj.com/articles/SB10001424052702304367204579270381937322174.

11 *Smith v. Maryland* is a 1979 Supreme Court case about a purse-snatcher caught when police obtained the suspect's phone records. It ruled that a telephone service provider's records of a customer's telephone activity – e.g. the fact that a call happened, the phone numbers involved, the duration of the call, but not the actual content of the call – do not implicate the Fourth Amendment.

5

Security, Terror, and Freedom:
The Dynamics of Public Opinion
in the French Surveillance Debate

Olivier Baisnée and Frédéric Nicolas

In July 2013, as the Snowden case unfolded and revelations about France's active cooperation in the US National Security Agency surveillance programme came to light, significant percentages of the French public objected to government surveillance practices.[1] In one YouGov poll, 43% of those surveyed said the French secret services were wrong to access personal communications data and 46% thought the *way in which information was gathered* was unjustified. Crucially, at that time, 58% felt that the surveillance programme had been used for purposes other than national security. A third of respondents supported granting political asylum to Edward Snowden.

Almost two years later, in April 2015, polls presented a very different picture of French public opinion. In the aftermath of the *Charlie Hebdo* terrorist attacks of January 2015,[2] a clear majority (63%) declared that they were in favour of 'measures that would enhance national security *even if that would mean a limitation of individual liberties on the internet*'. Similarly, 61% considered a new bill granting greater surveillance powers (then being drafted) an essential tool for identifying terrorists. Two out of three accepted the idea that individual's internet browsing data could be automatically surveilled. Unsurprisingly, the most willing supporters of enhanced surveillance were those less invested in internet use: elderly people, blue-collar workers, and mid-level employees. Young people were somewhat more critical but 47% of those aged 18–24 supported enhancing security at the expense of civil liberties.

The trend predictably continued after Paris suffered another round of deadly terrorist attacks in November of the same year.[3] By then, 84%

of those polled were 'ready to willingly accept more surveillance and a limitation of their individual liberties'. While only half of respondents trusted President François Hollande and his cabinet, 87% said they 'trusted the police [*police* and *gendarmerie*] and the intelligence services to face and fight terrorism'. In a subsequent poll, the language of the questions grew tougher – the more specific '*limitation* of individual liberties on the internet' became the much more broad '*willingly accepting* limitation of individual liberties' and in other places, the survey authors explicitly juxtaposed trust in the police against trust in the government. Still, at the end of 2015, 75% of French citizens said they were 'inclined toward the arrest and detention of people monitored for alleged terrorist activities [stating that] the State could not take so great a risk at the moment'.

This chapter sets key parts of the Snowden media coverage in France into the larger context of evolving attitudes among the French public on national security and civil liberties in the wake of the deadly terror attacks of 2015. Indeed, the terror attacks and the discourse they gave rise to in France significantly altered the discussion of surveillance tied to the Snowden leaks. There had been unfolding legal and political discourse at the fringes of French politics even before the Snowden revelations, but we argue that the Snowden affair was never explicitly linked to this discourse or the related political process. In the immediate aftermath of the leaks, the mainstream public debate took place mostly in *Le Monde*, with a single dominant frame, which emphasised shared global concern over US surveillance. Key politicians in France remained aloof in the debate. The terrorist attacks, however, dramatically reshaped the public and political landscape and, as a result, the opponents of surveillance largely disappeared from newspaper columns.

Our sample of the French mainstream media's opinion-based coverage is characterised, then, by two phases during which there was – albeit in different ways – no genuine public controversy on surveillance, which suggests journalists and the public missed an opportunity to more fully consider what the Snowden revelations meant and what should be done politically about the questions they raised. This is not to say there was no critical debate about the revelations in French public discourse. It does suggest, however, that, due to the structure of French journalism and the mediated public sphere, as well as to the unpredictable nature of events, the French national press missed a chance to explore with the public key concepts underpinning French media operations and the legitimacy of those concepts. The concrete political consequences of this process have been dramatic and continue to be far-reaching.

The old habits of secrecy and spying

France has a long tradition of state-sponsored surveillance. The pre-Revolution absolute monarchy was obsessed with spying on its critics (Darnton, 2011; Farge, 1992). In the eighteenth century, when 'public opinion' first emerged as a potential threat to the authorities, low standards of living made surveillance easier among the poor, who were most exposed to scrutiny (Farge, 1986). The lack of privacy was all the more damaging for the lower social classes because personal reputation was often the only capital a person could rely on to get a job, find a spouse, and to succeed in a suburban or rural world of social networks where interpersonal ties were vital.

It comes as no surprise, then, that in Louis-Sébastien Mercier's famous *Tableau de Paris* (1781–8), the King's informers ('les mouches du Roi') were mocked as the most despised elements of the Parisian population. The power elite hired these spies to eavesdrop and collect news circulating publicly hand-to-hand ('nouvelles à la main') in the streets, marketplaces, and taverns. The reports – which brimmed with libel, falsehoods, and mockery of the King and the royal family – were collected and scrutinised by authorities seeking to head off insurrection.

Such surveillance did not end with the French Revolution. During the Revolution, a regime of general suspicion (*loi des suspects*) and scrutiny prevailed. After the Revolution, the trend was amplified by the rapid development of the newspaper proto-industry on the one hand, and a complex system of state informers (prefects) on the other (Popkin, 1989). Two centuries passed and, in the late 1980s, President François Mitterrand (through his agents) was wiretapping those he suspected might reveal his personal secrets – his secret lover and their daughter, his troubling wartime past, his health issues, and so on. In the 2000s, the so-called 'Affaire des Fadettes' and 'Affaire Tarnac', the spying on *Le Monde* journalists and left-wing activists, demonstrate that, all the way to the Snowden revelations, the French intelligence services kept the old tradition of surveillance very much alive.[4]

It therefore comes as little surprise that those advocating for civil liberties in the aftermath of the Snowden revelations regularly referred to this historical background:

> *How can one imagine secret services showing appropriate restraint? Our Republic is getting ready to trample on its basic principles, without a glimpse of political dissent. The now well-known 'black boxes' of internet providers will be the exact replica of the 'cabinets noirs de l'Ancien Régime'. Thus, we ask the constitutional council for the bill on surveillance to be rejected as it is a violation to both the separation of powers and the right to privacy. (Le Monde, 26 June 2015)*

Indeed, even though the long tradition of state surveillance in France is woven into the fabric of civic life and on some level taken for granted by the public, the topic has attracted renewed publicity in the aftermath of the Snowden–NSA leaks. While digital technologies and their impact on privacy have rarely been debated in France, the Snowden case and the legislative proposal on surveillance passed in July 2015 after long debate prompted a new discourse in the French press. What makes the French case particularly interesting is how this discourse changed dramatically between 2013, when the Snowden leaks became public, and 2015, when deadly terrorist attacks were visited upon the French capital. In this unstable discursive space, we find disturbing evidence concerning the dynamics of public discussion and the crafting of the limits of legitimate controversy. We see journalists proposing contradictory definitions of the concept of 'public opinion' and using poll figures to bolster their arguments. While state surveillance has always reflected the anxiety of the political authorities about public opinion,[5] the Snowden episode suggests a different relationship between 'public opinion' and surveillance. In a curious historical twist, the former is used to justify the legalisation of the latter.

Two discourses, four phases

During 2013 and 2015, two parallel discourses formed in the French public debate – one about surveillance and the other about Snowden. They can be illustrated by the following editorial excerpts.

Le Monde considers that the public must not be kept ignorant of wire-tapping and surveillance programmes which are assuming such dimensions as to destroy any principle of democratic checks and balances. Our approach is not to uphold or to practice absolute transparency, which would consist in publishing all the data about everything, in its totality and irresponsibly. The 'Snowden revelations' are not aimed at weakening democratic societies but at strengthening them, promoting awareness of the risks this vast data search implies for our values, as it enables our lives, our contacts and our opinions to be read like an open book. (*Le Monde*, 21 October 2013)

The French are understandably jittery after the Paris and Tunis attacks, and they are alarmed by the radicalization of some in France who have fallen prey to jihadist recruitment on the internet. There is no doubt that the French government has a duty to protect the nation from terrorist violence and jihadist recruitment. But Parliament has a duty to protect citizens' democratic rights from unduly expansive and intrusive government surveillance. French lawmakers should not approve the bill unless judges are given a proper role in authorizing government surveillance, vague definitions of what constitutes a terrorist threat are struck from the bill and freedom of the press is protected. (*New York Times*, 31 March 2015)

These two quotes, originating from both sides of the Atlantic and from two different moments of the coverage, largely summarise the surveillance debate in France. While *Le Monde* in 2013 embarked on what resembled crusade journalism – devoting a lot of editorial space to the Snowden case – another discourse was in progress. This discourse aimed at enhancing the surveillance capabilities of the intelligence community, but it received little public attention. While the bill on surveillance had indeed been prepared and discussed for more than two years in Parliament, it was not brought into full view at the height of the NSA revelations but only after the terrorist attacks. Ironically, then, criticism of this major political shift in the French state's surveillance practices had to come, like a boomerang, from the US media.

To situate the Snowden episode within the public discourses of security and surveillance, it is useful to review the general articulation of these themes in the French press starting from March 2012, the period before the Snowden leaks were made public, to December 2015, the month after terrorist bombings rocked Paris. For some time before the Snowden revelations, both the French intelligence services and a few politicians had had their own security and surveillance agenda. This dates back to at least March 2012, when the intelligence services failed to prevent Mohamed Merah from killing three servicemen in Toulouse and Montauban, and three children and a teacher at a Jewish school in Toulouse. Merah had apparently been using the web both to prepare his attack and to disseminate propaganda.

Figure 5.1 shows search hits for the keywords 'surveillance' and 'Snowden', in *Le Monde*, *Le Figaro*, and *Libération*. The figure visualises two discourses that never really overlapped. The former was related to the surveillance bill, especially the need to legalise some well-known but unofficial secret practices targeting digital communications. Most notably, these included IMSI-catchers (to collect all data passing through mobile phones in a given area) and 'black boxes' – algorithms to monitor data traffic and terrorist activities. The latter discourse stemmed directly from the Snowden case. It was shaped by concerns about the protection of whistle-blowers, as voiced by experts in computing and activists for digital civil liberties (such as La Quadrature du Net, Génération Libre).

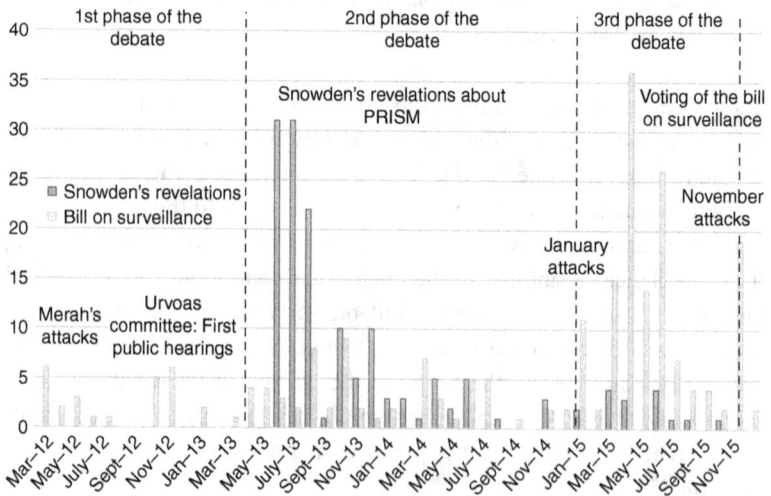

Figure 5.1 Comparison of coverage of the Snowden revelations and the surveillance bill in the three main national newspapers (*Le Monde, Le Figaro, Libération*). Y axis: Number of all stories (news, editorials, opinion material); searchword: 'Snowden'.

Both discourses addressed issues of privacy, but they were largely separate from each other, as indicated by Figure 5.1.[6]

Figure 5.1 shows that the traditional media coverage of the Snowden revelations was quite brief. It seems to have been more significant on the web, as one might expect from topics related to digital civil liberties. Organisations such as La Quadrature du Net and digital newspapers such as *Mediapart* (see Figure 5.2) were particularly engaged in the alternative coverage, but their views were hardly taken into account by public actors and civil servants debating the surveillance bill.

As a non-profit organisation, La Quadrature du Net was among the most proactive actors in the debate, defending the rights and freedom of citizens on the internet both online and in traditional media. For example, *Le Monde* quoted Jérémie Zimmermann, the organisation's spokesperson, in a piece on whistle-blowers that also referred to other major figures such as Christopher Soghoian, Jacob Appelbaum, Julian Assange, and, of course, Edward Snowden. Zimmermann's line of advocacy centres on the adaptation of legislation based in the founding principles of the internet, especially the free circulation of knowledge. Although he also encourages the general public to engage in the debate, he sees politics as the key to solving the problem of mass surveillance (through open legislative debate).

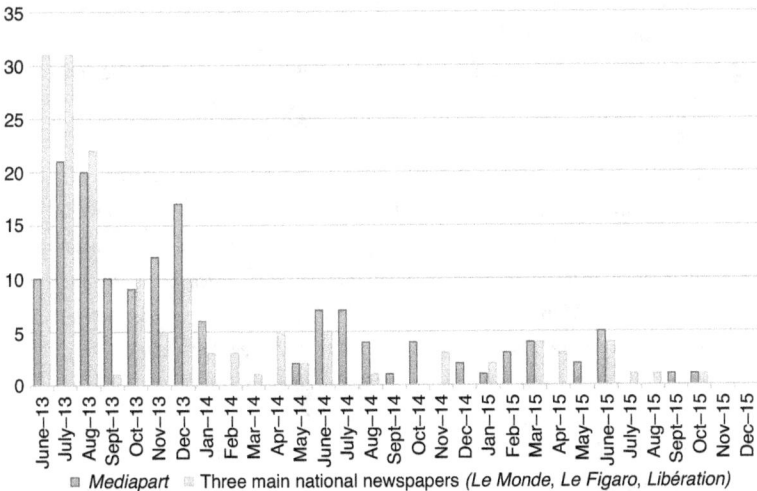

Figure 5.2 Comparison of coverage of the Snowden revelations in the three main national newspapers and *Mediapart*. Y axis: Number of all stories (news, editorials, opinion material); searchword: 'Snowden'.

He also promotes an alternative vision of the information technology industry, arguing for free software as well as for hardware free of data-harvesting features:

> We have to implement our solutions in the real world and everybody must be involved. We must start with the countries that are the most politically willing to get it started. We also have to catch up with free hardware since hackers have only focused on free software until now. This is a mistake. We haven't been tough enough with big IT companies, whose commercial strategies rely on the massive gathering and control of personal data through new devices. As a consequence, today, our smartphones have more to do with spying devices than with devices that allow us to make phone calls. (Le Monde, 11 December 2013)

Another example of alternative journalism is the purely online project *Mediapart*. It was created by former *Le Monde* chief editor Edwy Plenel and three other journalists (François Bonnet, Gérard Desportes, and Laurent Mauduit). *Mediapart* dedicated as much editorial space to the Snowden revelations as the three main national newspapers combined: *Mediapart* published 149 items; *Le Monde*, *Le Figaro*, and *Libération* combined published 149. The main frame of *Mediapart*'s coverage was the need for an independent press and for source protection to safeguard journalism and democracy from compromise. As Edwy Plenel argued in one of the first in-depth pieces dedicated to the case on *Mediapart*:

> To our readers, I deeply apologise for the length of this article. Here is why it is so long: We have to get away from the frenzy of day-to-day news in order to put into perspective what happened not only to Edward Snowden but also to Bradley Manning and Julian Assange. Since the launch of Mediapart in March 2008, we have defended the idea that the internet can convey more than superficial content. We see the internet as a powerful tool for journalism and therefore democracy. The comparison between our coverage of the Snowden revelations and the way they have been covered by what used to be considered the country's flagship news outlet (Le Monde) speaks for itself. While we believe we have arrived at a crucial moment for journalism and democracy, Le Monde is still merely counting points in the diplomatic battle between the US and Russia. (*Mediapart*, 15 December 2013)

Neither La Quadrature du Net nor *Mediapart* were influential enough to significantly influence the mainstream discourse of surveillance practices or to shape public opinion. This was true during the initial Snowden coverage and even more so following the 2015 terrorist attacks (see Figure 5.2).

Figures 5.1 and 5.2 help to identify four phases of the French media coverage. The first surveillance phase received little media attention. This corresponds to the first round of legislative talks about the legal framework of surveillance, commencing after the Merah attacks and, in particular, after the beginning of public hearings under the Urvoas committee in September 2012.[7] The low-grade debate continued until 2015 when, in the wake of the *Charlie Hebdo* killings and the November terrorist attacks, the issue resurfaced as an emergency, and the long-controversial surveillance law was passed within two weeks.

The second phase started with the Snowden revelations. Although at first broadly covered by the press, the case also receded quickly. During this second phase, the NSA surveillance practices (and the collaboration of the French intelligence services and IT companies) were heavily criticised for threatening privacy and the fundamental rights of citizens. Despite consistent coverage from June to September 2013, the media discourse lacked any real debate. The discussion mainly presented criticism of exposed US intelligence practices, while French politicians and authorities remained mostly absent from the debate – even though, as noted above, a small group of MPs was at that time drafting the new surveillance bill. A likely explanation is that the immediate public attention to the Snowden revelations made it too risky for MPs involved in the legislative process to go public. The (obviously unforeseen) 2015 attacks, on the other hand, created fertile soil in which to make arguments for greater security powers and did in fact produce favourable public opinion that helped quickly pass the law.

The third phase of the debate occurred in the days following the attacks in January 2015 on *Charlie Hebdo* and the Kosher grocery store in Paris. Until then, the discourses on the NSA and the surveillance legislation had remained largely unconnected. From then on, even general criticisms of surveillance disappeared completely from the mainstream opinion columns. The surveillance bill suddenly became a top priority for the government. After moving quietly through the parliamentary works for two years, the proposal seemed suddenly to burst fully formed onto centre stage and was embraced by a large majority of lawmakers who, supported by news media consensus, could claim that opinion polls clearly demonstrated the will of the people.

The fourth phase of the debate has unfolded in the months after the November 2015 attacks in Paris. The ethical issues and stakes raised by digital surveillance, already dwarfed by that year's first-wave terror attacks, were now completely discarded in the name of security. The absence was highlighted by the fact that discourse on surveillance and public opinion was being framed by the emergency anti-terror legislation that dramatically changed the conditions for enforcement of surveillance provisions. Under the new law, the intelligence services benefit from expanded police and judicial powers that come with little oversight. These powers were first set for a period of two months but have since been renewed many times. At one point, they were on the verge of becoming part of constitutional law. Although dropped at the last minute, this came close to consolidating the exceptional powers as status quo.

The 2015 terrorist attacks enabled the French intelligence services to advance their institutional interests along lines established by the NSA, as revealed by Snowden. The critical difference, of course, is that in France the practices were embraced openly, with wide support among elected officials and members of the public – and in the absence of significant criticism. The fact that the proposals enjoyed wide public support is both predictable and surprising. On one side, members of the public clearly were desperate for change. The intelligence services had just failed for the third time in two years to prevent terrorist attacks (or the fifth time, depending on whether you count the attempted August 2015 bombing of the Thalys train and the May 2014 stabbing at the Jewish museum in Brussels). So, on the other side, and for the same reasons, the agencies had earned some measure of public distrust or at least lack of confidence. Indeed, even as the agencies struggled to develop digital security strategies, terrorists posted videos of the attacks on social networks such as Twitter and French jihadists in Syria continued to send video 'postcards' abroad and appear as interview subjects with mainstream journalists using Skype.

Key actors: the structure of public space

In addition to laying out the evolution of the debate, it is also worth illustrating the discursive structure of the debates by describing the main categories of actors involved. Four major parties to the debate can be identified: intelligence agency staffers, politicians, journalists, and members of the general public. These should not be seen as internally homogeneous or mutually exclusive groups. In the debate around the surveillance bill, some political actors endorsed the claims of the intelligence services, but the vast majority of politicians did not participate. Similarly, the level of involvement on the part of French journalists in promoting the issue and fuelling debate varied across the field.

As part of the discourse, the intelligence services mainly acted to advance institutional interests. Less apparent was an openness to develop new broader views and approaches in light of the dramatically evolving threat. As a result, electronic surveillance has increasingly become the domain of a particular segment of the intelligence services (mobilised around these issues worldwide), rather than an issue to be explored primarily in the public square. Bauman et al. (2014) have argued that this contributes to a profound redefinition of the fundamental basis of international relations. The result is that the public is removed further from policy-making tied to national security, because the role of publicly elected officials decreases as the role of unelected intelligence agency bureaucrats expands.

A group of participants in the public debate coalesced around Jean-Jacques Urvoas, who was a key player in preparing the surveillance bill. They were known mainly as 'second-tier' politicians who supported providing a legal framework around the intelligence services. Only a limited number of politicians ever directly participated in the debate, in part because of the lack of technical expertise, but also because internet-related issues – including internet regulation and governance – have been generally absent from French political debate. Indeed, the last two presidential campaigns saw no change in this regard. French politicians typically have only betrayed the thinnest ties to digital technology. Presidents François Hollande and Nicolas Sarkozy did not use computers at all; Hollande has been mocked for writing his Twitter messages on paper to be copied onto the web, and Sarkozy's aides maintain his Facebook page.

When internet issues are taken into account in governmental and parliamentary activities, emphasis has mainly been placed on preserving business interests tied to copyright issues and safeguarding national security in the face of new digital threats, such as cyberterrorism, cyberwar, and cyber-crime.

French journalists have a particular sensitivity to surveillance issues because of recent history.[8] Journalists are also heavy users of digital devices for professional and personal reasons, and therefore are major potential targets for surveillance. This can also be understood as a form of digital *ethnocentrism*, where journalists tend to universalise their very distinct position in regard to the issues at stake. This has to date mostly meant that journalists have sided with the defenders of fundamental civil rights and liberties, a position that has not incurred any real political price. In addition, the very proactive role played by *Le Monde* in reporting the Snowden stories must be understood in the context of the paper's general strategy to position itself among the world's top global investigative newspapers.[9] The political price of this sensitivity to civil rights issues, however, changed with the terrorist attacks of 2015 and the heightened national security politics that followed.

The second phase of the debate also included the participation of a handful of experts and civic organisations. Members voiced concern about NSA practices, first advocating for greater transparency on the part of the government, then for the protection of whistle-blowers (with an eye towards Snowden's effectively forced exile in Russia), and finally for greater general public awareness of the seriousness of the issue and the need to act on it. Again, the terrorist attacks and the shift in public opinion effected a shift in the debate and the positions of these actors, reducing the newsworthiness of some of the arguments being made by external contributors to the coverage, such as La Quadrature du Net and Génération Libre.

As is usually the case, the general public was spoken for and much spoken about, but few members of the general public took part in the mediated debate itself (cf. Bourdieu, 1973: 1292–1309). In addition, the esoteric nature of the topic purportedly distanced citizens from the debate rather than encouraging them to participate. The press (and the few highly specialised actors involved in the debate) have tended to objectify the general public, relying on an image of 'normal users' as mostly digitally illiterate. In this way, debate about the consequences of surveillance for democracy remained confined, limited to abstract concepts (individual liberties, privacy) rather than touching on the daily lives of the vast majority of citizens. In the wake of the 2015 terrorist attacks, there was also perceived to be massive public support for decisions with more concrete objectives: ensuring security, stopping terrorists, and preventing new attacks and radicalisation.

From no debate – to no debate

In the opinionated coverage published in the three main national newspapers in France, we note the first significant difference between *Le Monde* on one side and *Libération* and *Le Figaro* on the other, in both analytical reporting and distinctly opinion material.[10]

Often anachronistically depicted in the international literature as a newspaper close to the authorities, *Le Monde*'s recent history has been characterised by a clear shift in editorial policy. During the 1990s, the director, Jean-Marie Colombani, and the editor-in-chief, Edwy Plenel, developed a new tradition of investigative journalism. During Sarkozy's presidency, the paper was a main outlet for breaking news, including political scandal. Authorities spied on *Le Monde* reporters and monitored their relationships with anti-corruption judges. The government snooping was at the centre of the 'Affaire des Fadettes', in which it came out that the French secret service obtained detailed phone records tying *Le Monde* reporters to their judicial sources. The case engendered debate, especially in *Le Monde*, over source protection. The case worked in effect to sensitise *Le Monde* staff to issues of government surveillance, tilling the ground for the Snowden stories.

More recently, under the direction of Nathalie Nougayrède (now at the *Guardian*), *Le Monde* has developed a two-pronged strategy. On the one hand, it tries to actively manage the digital evolution of the newspaper by hiring new journalists who are keen to work online, and by completely reorganising its website. On the other hand, it seeks to become a player in the global media landscape through active participation in international investigations. This model is reminiscent of the *Guardian* strategy and, along with its active collaboration in the international consortium of investigative journalists working on leaked documents (WikiLeaks, NSA, OffshoreLeaks, etc.), serves to explain why the *Le Monde* has placed such emphasis on the issue. Its main goal was to be the 'first global French-speaking media outlet'.[11]

From this perspective, *Le Monde*'s involvement in major investigations across the world published in different media comes as little surprise. On the contrary, the Snowden story fits perfectly with the paper's larger editorial vision, in that it is both global and investigative. Rubbing shoulders with some of the most prestigious outlets around the world is an effective way for the paper to assert its own legitimacy and trumpet its high standards. It also helps to explain why *Le Monde* devoted much more editorial space to the debate around Snowden and the NSA than to the 2015 surveillance legislation (and why *Le Monde* was the main target of government surveillance under Sarkozy's presidency).

In exploring the debate – the actual reaction to Snowden's revelations from June 2013 to April 2014 – we identified five major themes through which the mainstream media framed their opinionated coverage. First, the most common way of framing the issue was to demand legal oversight to propose or pass laws that would monitor internet surveillance. This was often suggested at the national level, but in the French debate, arguments were also advanced for transnational rules (European and beyond).

> *How much illegal phone tapping are the operators doing for the French secret services (DGSE)? Does it solely concern international communications? What about the information collected? Do the French services keep it, or is it given to or exchanged with allied countries? What is the nature of the relationship with the National Security Agency (NSA)? … Our citizens should now be informed about what is at stake here, and measures should be implemented to regulate the activities of the secret services in order to protect our private lives and fundamental freedom.* (*Le Monde*, 23 April 2014)

Second, the revelations provoked a specifically European discourse about the need for Europe to develop a global industrial strategy on media technology, taking advantage of the fact that the reputations of both the US and its main opponents, Russia and China, were at stake. The idea that Europe might offer an alternative policy was discussed more widely in Europe too but it was well illustrated by the French debate.

> *There is not enough parliamentary and public debate; there is a lack of enlightened criticism in the media, and a poorly structured independent assessment of these matters in the European Union. Those who are not 'digital natives' should understand that technology is not only the prerogative of geeks. Indeed, digital technology has become a tool in the battle for power, involving close collaboration between public and private actors. Europe has to overcome these weaknesses in order to be one of internet's major industrial and political poles. What is at stake for Europeans is to manage to converge their digital diplomacies to gain political and economic importance among the USA and the major emerging countries.* (*Le Figaro*, 2 October 2013)

Third, the debate focused in part around journalism and the question of the legal protections journalists and their sources should expect to enjoy. Debate around this theme included arguments for providing asylum to Snowden, the legal rights of whistle-blowers, and the need to foster more investigative journalism (especially the need to exploit big data). These arguments commonly overlapped with calls for government transparency, exemplified by a joint opinion piece by Julian Assange and Christophe Deloire published in *Le Monde*.

> *Big Brother is watching us from Washington's suburbs. The institutions that make American democracy possible have to face their responsibility and act as a counter-power to the executive power and the Patriot Act ... The Whistleblower Protection Act must be amended in order to efficiently protect those who act for the general interest.* (*Le Monde*, 4 July 2013)

The revelations also provoked concerns about surveillance focused on particular institutions or that threatened professional boundaries of trust.

> *If a system of mass gathering of French citizens' data existed, it would be 'a-legal.' The National Commission on Informatics and Liberty (CNIL) has the right to monitor the data collected by intelligence services and the police, at the citizen's request ... The data from the secret services and from the military Intelligence services currently have a derogatory status [that prevent us from accessing it]. It would be a rightful claim if the CNIL was asking to monitor this data, in respect of both democracy and military secrecy. The Snowden revelations could help defend our case.* (*Le Monde*, 24 October 2013)

A number of stories viewed the incident mostly through the lens of international politics, as a diplomatic story and as a geopolitical story about the power play at work among the nations involved.

> *The plot twists in the escape of Edward Snowden, the American IT specialist who revealed the Prism cyber surveillance programme, highlights the new worldwide cold war that is about to start. The fate of a single person cannot transform international relationships, even if that person possesses special information that can potentially harm the interests of the USA. However, the way in which Russian and Chinese propaganda are using his case is a sign of a new rivalry between Washington, Moscow*

and Beijing, reminiscent of times when there was a confrontation between the Soviet Union and the 'free world' … Chinese propaganda has on this occasion overtaken that of Russia. It is questioned by Washington because Snowden fled to Hong Kong. For The People's Daily, the USA has gone from being 'models of human rights' to 'spies of private lives', 'manipulators' of the power centralised on the internet and mad 'invaders' of the networks of third-party countries. (Le Figaro, 2 June 2013)

Finally, the 'ordinary citizen' also figured (though less prominently than other actors) in framing the issue. In particular, there were calls for more media literacy, stressing the need for citizens to be more aware of how their digital practices can expose them to surveillance. The arguments advocated for free software and new encryption techniques, often citing hackers and whistle-blowers as role models of concerned citizenry.

If Edward Snowden is teaching us anything, it is that it is high time to regain control over computer science. The ball lies in our court. Either we can ignore the warning he has just given us by putting his life at risk, or we can start a new and more mature relationship with computers rather than remaining passive consumers. … It is not easy to regain control over computer science, but it is an essential citizen initiative. Free software should be everyone's priority. (Libération, 25 February 2014)

The most active and visible contributors to the opinion pieces during the initial Snowden debate were journalists themselves, followed by academics and intellectuals. Experts from civil society and the private sector also contributed their views, as did various civil servants. In contrast, there were minimal contributions from major politicians and representatives of the intelligence community to the actual Snowden debate.

As previously noted, the second phase of the debate (see Figure 5.1) was exceptional by comparison with the other three. Although attention to digital surveillance practices seemed to peak in this phase, with the involvement of many stakeholders, the exchanges lacked rigorous or even lively public and *political* debate that would have fostered controversy and underlined conflicting interests. Instead, there was passing consensus on the need to monitor surveillance. This phase of the debate can be characterised as a shadow-boxing form of advocacy. It involved only a few specialised professionals – either those whose task was to monitor surveillance (including elected politicians, appointed civil servants, IT companies, and civil rights activists) – or those who were targeted by surveillance in their work (journalists, hackers). In addition, the debate involved those who were merely analysing the situation (academics and intellectuals, especially in the fields of law, international relations, security, and political philosophy). This chorus of voices was mostly unanimous, while no concerns were voiced, for instance, by the general public. Pierre Alonso, of *Libération,* underlined:

> *The fact that political struggle is tied to technical skills is not good news. Those who are not skilled won't be as safe as those with the right skills. Nobody wants to create a technical 'aristocratie,' a technocracy protected from mass surveillance, when others would not be able to evade it. A lot is now being done to make the means to escape surveillance accessible to the general public. This is highly laudable as long as nobody forgets the political stakes – that is, the struggle against all forms of mass surveillance.* (*Libération,* 25 July 2015)

Consequently, the initial Snowden debate largely focused on technical or specialised issues, as opposed to wide and open debate on democracy and citizen rights in the digital age (Abbott, 1988). Professionals from the intelligence community remained outside this phase of the debate. The occasional politicians who became involved were relatively discreet, compared to latter phases when their legislative activity came to the fore. At this point, they skilfully hijacked the need for monitoring as advocated, moving the discussion into one about the need to legalise surveillance. The main line of argument among those promoting the surveillance bill related to the need to provide new means of action and to legalise existing practices. That legal framework was repeatedly presented as a precondition for monitoring. The ethical aspect of surveillance – whether or not it was morally acceptable – was not a major concern. Surveillance was presented as unavoidable.

At the high point of the Snowden debate, during 2013 and 2014, one can say that public discourse represents an 'epiphenomenon' – a parallel and secondary debate that seems to touch on the ongoing discussion of security and surveillance in France but fails to exploit the revelations and fully activate the issue. Rather than constructing a 'public' that features genuine disagreement around possible trade-offs and policy alternatives, the debate tended to emphasise the obstacles that would prevent the emergence of a multi-voiced and interactive open debate.

Conclusion

Overall, the long arch of the Snowden debate in the French mainstream news media seems to cover surprisingly narrow territory. While occasionally thoughtful, it seemed mostly displaced and disconnected from both the ongoing legislative politics of surveillance and the experience of everyday life. It provided only few prolific media professionals the opportunity to voice their concerns about surveillance. These figures seemed satisfied to reassert their power over their professional jurisdictions, limiting control over discourse to a small number of highly skilled individuals and specialised organisations.

In a sense, the French case can be summarised as a discursive shift from one kind of 'no debate' to another kind of 'no debate'. In the first stage, this disconnect occurred between the revelations and discussion of the surveillance bill. The political energy of the journalistic revelations seems to have no equivalent in the political field. While we cannot conclusively point here to any conscious strategy on the part of the intelligence community or the political elite that failed to join the first wave of the Snowden coverage, it seems clear that the first phase reflects the particular field constellation inside French journalism and between the journalistic and political fields. The active involvement of Le Monde can be seen as part of its new global strategy and politics. The inactivity of other papers, on the other hand, reflects their reluctance to participate in discourse production dominated by their professional competitor. In addition to these *internal* field relations within journalism, then, the first disconnection reflects the *external* power of the political field – the capacity of political actors to remain detached from an issue they consider potentially toxic. Encouraged by public opinion polls in the first phase, the silence of the political elite in the media acted to effectively manage the public sphere. An international enemy was identified in the debate, and there was little incentive for the political elite to step into the public minefield by connecting ongoing discussion of the surveillance bill with the Snowden case.

After the terrorist attacks the media agenda altered completely, as did mediated public opinion. There was no longer any option for political actors to avoid entering the media discourse. At this point, the context of the debate changed. If the public 'enemy' of the initial stage of the debate was the surveillance machinery of the US (and UK), it was now everywhere, forcing the country into both a technical and intellectual state of emergency. At such moments, the political field transforms from a *passively* powerful to an *actively* powerful force. The activity of the political field usually broadens the capacity for journalism to manoeuvre, as political differences open a space for controversies and opposing interpretations. In this case, the national security argument, however, fixated the discourse in a 'no debate' state before it had even properly begun to reshape. Defending freedom and free speech, paradoxically, transformed into an argument for enhancing surveillance.

The last-minute amendment of the bill (named 'Amendement Edward Snowden'), which was supposed to protect whistle-blowers in the secret services, was withdrawn by the French Parliament in the summer of 2015. Journalists are far from protected by the new law, as it seems doubtful that the right to protect sources would be taken seriously against the consensus regarding the need for digital surveillance at the expense to whatever degree of civil liberties. Take, for instance, Prime Minister Valls' reasoning for a constitutional bill eventually passed by the French National Assembly on 11 February 2016:

> Giving the State the means to protect the Nation from terrorism and fanaticism, while preserving the values of the Republic, is awaited by all French citizens. To that end, a modification of the Constitution is now necessary. Every French man and woman should be able to gather around that shared ambition.[12]

As we write this conclusion, Snowden's revelations are fading in the public memory and moving out of the news cycle. The modification of the French constitution to include the state of emergency security powers – although abandoned by François Hollande – has received support from MPs from the far left to the middle right. Ironically, while the call to strip terrorists of their French nationality originated from Front National, their MPs voted against this measure. At the same time, the bill also drew fierce opposition, dividing the major political parties and even provoking the resignation of Christiane Taubira, the Minister of Justice. However, the intense political debate did not even then focus on the state of emergency measures or extension of police powers. Rather, it focused on the symbolic measure of stripping terrorists of their nationality.

On 22 January 2016, French prime minister Manuel Valls declared that the emergency state would be extended until 'we get rid of ISIS', and Jean-Jacques Urvoas, instigator of the surveillance law, was appointed Minister of Justice. A third terror attack, in Nice (14 July 2016), occurred during Valls' premiership. In the context of the forthcoming (2017) presidential elections this provoked a new wave of demands for strict security means. Still, the hard work of those in power seems to have been politically in vain: Hollande has decided not to run and Valls has lost the socialist party primaries. Polls predict a political disaster to the ruling party (8-10% at the first row). As we write the final sentence to this story so far (February 2017) the conservative François Fillon seems set to face Marine Le Pen in the second round of the elections. In all probability, this paves the way to an even harder attack on civil liberties.

Notes

1 YouGov for the Huffington Post (French edition): http://cdn.yougov.com/cumulus_uploads/document/2x87lx33er/baro_politique_HP_Jul.pdf (accessed Dec. 2015).

2 CSA for Atlantico. www.atlantico.fr/decryptage/63-francais-favorables-limitation-libertes-individuelles-pour-lutter-contre-terrorisme-yves-marie-cann-2089085.html (accessed Dec. 2015).

3 IFOP for *Le Figaro* and www.rtl.fr/actu/societe-faits-divers/attentats-a-paris-les-francais-favorables-a-une-certaine-limitation-des-libertes-7780543321 (accessed Dec. 2015).

4 'Affaire des Fadettes' refers to the surveillance of journalists (and their sources) who were investigating potential scandals during Sarkozy's Presidency. 'Affaire de Tarnac' refers to a case where a group of leftist activists living in a village in south-west France were suspected of having organised a train sabotage and were monitored due to a supposed 'anarcho-autonomist' plan to undermine the Republic's institutions. This complex case remains at the judicial phase, but the actions of intelligence and police services against a supposed far-left terrorism plan has been widely debated.

5 To preserve social and political order in the first stage (eighteenth and nineteenth centuries) and, subsequently, when universal suffrage was instituted in the absence of opinion polls (until the 1960s), to reduce political uncertainty in France (Blondiaux, 1998).

6 The empirical materials were drawn from the Europresse database. The collection focused on words 'Snowden' and 'surveillance'.

7 Jean-Jacques Urvoas was then MP and President of the Law Committee at the French Assemblée Nationale. From an academic background, he has been a key player in the debate around surveillance practices and services, from 2012 onwards. He was appointed Minister of Justice in Feb. 2016.

8 On wiretapping in the 1980s, see Pontaut and Pontaut, 1996; Plenel, 1999, 2006. On the 'Affaire des Fadettes', see Davet and Lhomme, 2011.

9   *Le Monde* is one of the newspapers that had access to the Snowden files. It dedicated a special section of its website to the PRISM–NSA–Snowden case and published a series of articles translated into English. During the sampling period (June 2013 – Feb. 2014), *Le Monde* accounted for 70% of all published op-ed articles (73% of all articles) published by *Le Monde*, the *Guardian,* and the *New York Times.*

10 *Le Monde* is known to be a centre-left newspaper, read by French political elites and academics (298,992 copies sold in Oct. 2013). *Le Figaro* is known to be a conservative newspaper (333,342 copies sold in Oct. 2013). *Libération* is known to be a progressive left-wing newspaper (103,836 copies sold in Oct. 2013). We looked at items that mention 'NSA', 'N.S.A', 'Snowden', or 'Cybersurveillance' in their title, using the Europresse platform and the *Le Monde* website to collect our sample. The decision to focus primarily on *Le Monde* was motivated by its inclusion in the international consortium of newspapers allowed access to the Snowden files.

11 Nathalie Nougayrède, quoted in *L'Express*: http://www.lexpress.fr/actualite/nathalie-nougayrede-un-peu-seule-au-monde_1289837.html (accessed Dec. 2015).

12 Manues Valls (2015), Projet de loi N° 3381: 'Projet de loi constitutionnelle de protection de la Nation', http://www.assemblee-nationale.fr/14/projets/pl3381.asp (accessed Feb. 2017).

6

'Please Stay Frustrated!': The Politicisation of Digital Technologies in the German NSA Debate

Johanna Möller and Anne Mollen

'I will be satisfied', said Edward Snowden when providing the set of secret NSA documents to the wider public, 'if the federation of secret law, unequal pardon and irresistible executive powers that rule the world that I love are revealed for even an instant'.[1] Snowden's act of disclosing massive data collection by intelligence agencies was a political act pointing to illegal surveillance activities by states and businesses. The computer expert, hired by an NSA contractor, based his decision to disregard the rules of his professional, and in principle non-political, activity on the argument that civil rights were threatened and citizens should be aware of surveillance practices that heavily affect their privacy. Beyond this act of whistle-blowing, the NSA revelations also point to another political dimension as they bear the potential of supporting the politicisation of digital technologies in the wider public debate. As never before, the case revealed, on a broad scale, that private media use and security by digital surveillance are issues that call for public negotiation.

Even though technology as such was not the target of critique, Snowden has – for several years now – actively been calling for citizens to reclaim their privacy by using data encryption or secure technology. The intent of this chapter is to discuss this latter process of technology politicisation in the context of the German general public debate. At stake is whether and how technology turns into a politicised, that is, politically negotiable, issue in the course of the debate. The question is if there is a political action field that unfolds in the context of this debate.

The notion of politicisation points to a process during which an issue's definition and regulation is called into question and transported into the field of politics. Buzan, Wæver, and de Wilde provide a useful definition that hints at this process:

> *Politicisation means to make an issue appear to be open, a matter of choice, something that is decided upon and that therefore entails responsibility, in contrast to issues that either could not be different (laws of nature) or should not be put under political control (e.g., a free economy, the private sphere, and matters for expert decision).* (Buzan et al., 1998: 29)

When referring to politicisation it is necessary to point out which understanding of the political is implied. Zürn (2015: 167) roughly distinguishes two meanings of the concept: with reference to Aristotle, Tocqueville, and Habermas, the political denotes 'public debates about the right course in handling a collective problem' or, referring to Weber, Schmitt and Easton, the political points to 'the ability to make collectively binding decisions'. Both meanings, he argues, play a role in politicisation, as issues are moved 'into the realm of public choice, thus presupposing the possibility to make collectively binding decisions on that matter'. Based on a similar understanding, Buzan et al emphasise that politicisation is not necessarily a process that transports an issue from non-political (i.e., private or economic) fields to the political sphere. Politicisation explicitly also implies the destabilisation of political units, 'a collectivity that has gained a separate existence distinct from its subjects' (Buzan et al., 1998: 143).

It is important to keep this in mind when talking about the politicisation of technology that often yields disruptive effects on political units, such as the nation-state or the notion of democracy (Bauman et al., 2014). Thus, when it comes to the politicisation of technology, we need to keep in mind that it is not only about addressing an issue in the context of currently functional political units, but that these very political units might be called into question by matters related to the issue as well.

How can we analyse politicisation empirically? Here, we can benefit from Europeanisation research that specialises in politicisation processes in public debates (Risse, 2014; De Wilde et al., 2015). Yet Zürn points out how important it is to keep in mind that 'not all that receives media attention is political' (2015: 168). Europeanisation researchers draw on a three-dimensional analysis of politicisation in public debates: salience, expansion, and polarisation (see Risse, 2015; De Wilde and Zürn, 2012).

Salience refers to the increasing visibility of an issue. Thus, it results from increasing public attention given to a policy issue and specifying political, economic, or cultural stakes embedded in the topic. *Expansion* refers to the dispersion of a given issue across the political spectrum, articulated through diversity or actors drawn into (or allowed to access) the debate. *Polarisation* refers to the 'increasing contentiousness' of actors and arguments involved in a debate (Hooghe and Marks, 2012: 841). This means that different political projections regarding the future of dealing with a given issue result in rhetorical conflicts and contestations.

The NSA scandal can be regarded as a key disruptive moment in which digital technologies with their wide-ranging political implications were made very visible on the general public's agenda. Herein, the German media public, which traditionally highly values privacy and data security, serves as an illustrative example in order to tackle politicisation processes of digital technology in debates following the NSA revelations. Not least, the German case is interesting because the disclosures revealed, step by step, the tight entanglement of the German Secret Service (Bundesnachrichtendienst, BND) with the NSA and their cooperation in systematic surveillance.

In this chapter, we look at how the issue was discussed in the opinionated sections of German journalism, focusing on two leading, quality German newspapers, *Frankfurter Allgemeine Zeitung* (*FAZ*) and *Süddeutsche Zeitung* (*SZ*), both considered newspapers of record. *SZ* was selected because the paper in coalition with the German TV channel NDR continuously investigated the material leaked by Snowden and aired the first TV interview with the whistle-blower worldwide (after Glenn Greenwald and Laura Poitras). *FAZ*, on the other hand, is known for addressing current debates beyond day-to-day revelations by reflecting on larger societal implications.

Based on a large sampling of the entire NSA coverage, starting with the Snowden revelations, we selected three weeks with intense, peak periods for analysis. After the first, initial peak of the revelations (24–30 June 2013), the second one focused on the 'Merkel mobile affair', when Snowden's documents showed that the German chancellor's mobile phone had been eavesdropped (28 October–3 November 2013). The third period of intense coverage followed Barack Obama's public speech addressing the reform of US intelligence agencies policy (20–26 January 2014). During this time, the debate focused on Germany's domestic affairs. In sum, 69 opinionated articles were selected for closer analysis. Here, our main focus is to look at the presence, meandering, and political projections of digital technologies. In short, we want to understand how – and how politically – digital technology was framed in this German public debate.

Digital technologies as an issue in the German NSA coverage

In the sample of German opinionated coverage, we identified four thematic areas: (1) international relations, (2) citizens, (3) economy, and (4) future of democracy (Table 6.1). In each of these broad frames, questions about digital technology were articulated in different ways. In the context of international relations, digital technologies were seen to threaten the sovereignty of nation-states and questions were raised about the misuse of digital technologies by powerful states. Within the citizens' frame, digital technologies were seen as a means of *massive* surveillance and, thus, as a threat to citizens' privacy and security. In the field of economy, digital technologies were framed as resources and as tools in the hands of powerful economic actors, such as Facebook or Google. Finally, digital technologies were discussed with regard to the future of democracy. Viewpoints were highlighted that argued for the need for finding new ways of understanding and reinforcing democracy against the backdrop of current technological developments.

Based on the thematic analysis, we investigated the extent to which digital technologies gained *salience* in the debate. In each of the three peaks of coverage, we could see the presence of all the four thematic areas. Nonetheless, their status in the media debate varied over time.

Entering the political realm

At the beginning of the debate, directly following Snowden's disclosures, frames related to the themes of 'citizens' and 'international relations' dominated both newspapers. The revelation of NSA mass surveillance of citizens worldwide resulted in numerous comments on the enormous potential for the misuse of digital technologies. Technology, in these frames, appeared to be an instrument of illegal and/or illegitimate mass

Table 6.1 Frames of media technologies bundled according to thematic areas

Thematic area	Frames
International relations	Media technologies blur state borders and national sovereignty
	Dependence on foreign media technologies threatens national sovereignty
	Transnational character of media technologies and communication networks complicates and hinders regulation
	Exploiting media technologies' potential is an established tool in international espionage
	Misuse of the media technology by Americans threatens US–German relations
	Welfare as a means to upgrade secure national media technologies
	Investment into secure national media technologies as a future political challenge
Citizens	Media technologies enable massive Secret Service surveillance
	They can be used to violate citizens' privacy and freedom
	People can be measured by media technologies
	Media technology literacy as a civic duty of protection
	Citizens' duty to understand consequences of applying media technologies
Economics	Media technologies is a growing market
	Secure media technologies is a growing market
	Media technologies as a contract between users and companies
	Media technologies in the hands of powerful companies
Future of democracy	Media technologies represent ideas of (cyber)freedom
	Media technologies enable surveillance
	Developers of media technologies do not reflect societal implications
	Current societies witness demystification of media technologies
	Institutional regulation of media technologies is an illusion
	Political institutions and citizens need to find new ways and concepts to communicate
	Media technology as a key realm and instrument of state political action

surveillance in the hands of intelligence agencies and governments, which was being used against citizens. 'Unfortunately, any state can put its spoon into the electronic soup', argued Georg Mascolo, a prominent German journalist (*FAZ*, 26 June 2013). While Mascolo maintained that a sovereign state can and will use digital technologies for its interests, Constance Kurz, the spokesperson of the political hacking organisation Chaos Computer Club, claimed the contrary. For her, digital bulk surveillance proved that technologies have eroded the sovereign power of nation-states, and that the NSA case highlighted the failure of states to control digital technologies. Yet, 'in an age of global internet, communication sovereignty over one's own communication flows is paramount to governmental integrity and independence, let alone economic prosperity' (*FAZ*, 28 June 2013).

These insights point to the conclusion that technological infrastructure should be high on the political agenda, not just nationally but also internationally. In that context, a foreign correspondent of *SZ* described China's use of the revelations as a pretext to 'separate' its internet and data infrastructures from global communication flows, as well as to resist technologies developed in Western countries (*SZ*, 26 June 2013) (see also Chapters 7 and 8).

Parallel to this international relations-centred debate, citizens were addressed as a key political unit. On the one hand, citizens, and particularly their privacy, were portrayed as being sacrificed to massive surveillance. Similar to Mark Andrejevic's (2013) argument on Big Data's entrenchment with effective surveillance, many articles pointed to how people's use of digital technologies enables not only intelligence agencies but also economic actors to create detailed personal profiles (for instance, *SZ*, 26 June 2013). On the other hand, the commentaries highlighted citizens' possibilities for self-defence against violations of their privacy, arguing that it has become necessary to understand the consequences of technology use and to become more media literate. Articles explained, sometimes in great technical detail, how surveillance actually works and that people need to be wary about spreading their personal data (*FAZ*, 25 June 2013). From a more encompassing perspective, the media commentaries reflected citizens' disappointment prompted by the demystification of a free internet (*FAZ*, 29 June 2013). These insights demonstrate that digital technologies were addressed as an ambivalent issue from the beginning of the debate, and thus calling two political units into question: nation-states and citizens. Following the revelation of Angela Merkel's mobile phone wiretap, the focus shifted gradually more to international relations and specifically to a discussion of the troubled US–German relations. The wiretapping triggered a political scandal that resulted in persistent discussion of digital technologies and their role in international relations. In this context, the opinion pieces also reflected on digital surveillance as a normal element of international espionage. While a well-known German liberal politician, Christian Lindner, argued that the American government should not risk the German–American friendship by exploiting digital technologies just because they are able to generate massive amounts of data (*FAZ*, 28 October 2013), other observers described intelligence agencies garnering all the data they have access to – even from friendly states – as business as usual (*SZ*, 29 October 2013).

After it was revealed that Angela Merkel's phone had been intercepted, some articles also looked at the market's power to help with privacy protection. Secure digital technologies were portrayed as a growing market. It was noted that customers were now shifting their attention to investments into their individual privacy and data security. Yet opinions persisted that total protection from surveillance is an illusion. In an interview, Chris Dedicoat, CEO of CISCO, described the self-healing powers of the internet, which works as 'a catalyst for innovation, productivity, economic growth and societal development' (*FAZ*, 23 January 2014). He explained further that 'we head for a highly networked world that ... will result in the "ultra personalisation" of information, entertainment and services [pertaining to] ... automatic traffic control, the maintenance of buildings, and forward-thinking and truly democratic health care'. In saying so, Dedicoat assumed that digital technologies can handle democratic tasks in their own right – thereby promoting the de-politicisation of digital technologies as he ascribed the task of individual security both to the private and economic sphere.

In the third peak of intense coverage, the reporting occasionally highlighted that digital technologies will shape future societies and democracies in a revolutionary manner. These fundamental changes call for new ways of understanding democracy in the digital era. An often-made claim was that the future of democracy depends on new ideas for dealing with digital technologies outside the economic sphere. In this sense, Evgeny Morozov called for 'attacking the religion of data craving' (*FAZ*, 24 January 2014) and pointed towards the need for new political actors: 'In this debate, we depend on brilliant minds that understand both information technology and constitutional law'. One article in the *SZ* sketched out a European Convention on intelligence agencies as a reply to the fundamental ideological difference between Europe and the US concerning security and privacy. The solution, it was argued, would be to reorganise political institutions and companies to create technologies that operate in favour of the European understanding of privacy and security and a corresponding model of democracy (*SZ*, 23 January 2014).

In sum, the ambiguous and possibly transformative effects of technology were prominently represented in the German debate. Conversely, attempts to depoliticise technology, for instance via economic arguments, were rather few. Yet the way in which the politicisation of technology took place changed over time. At the time of the Merkel phone hacking affair, rather simple ideas of digital technologies as instruments in the hands of nation-states dominated; later, more fundamental discussions emerged, partly questioning established political actors and institutions, and also widely held concepts. In the face of the uncertainty over whether existing political institutions would be able to solve problems related to security and rights of individual citizens, we encounter both a differentiation of perspectives on digital technologies and competing visions of how to deal with the transformative processes that concern digital technologies. These two directions are analysed in the following sections.

Meandering within the political field

As we have seen, digital technologies were introduced as a politically relevant topic within a number of thematic areas. As the debate went on, we also observed an increasing *diversification* of frames *within* each of these themes. Therefore, in the next step, we focus specifically on the diverse framing of digital technologies as a concept, the political units that are addressed with reference to digital technologies and possible transformations in the ways established political actors were challenged. We do so by concentrating on all frames identified as being related to citizens' roles in the NSA reporting.

The beginning of the NSA scandal was marked by a focus on the citizens' need to take an active role regarding digital technologies. Given that trust in national governments and federal courts had diminished, it was argued that citizens must take privacy protection into their own hands

(*SZ*, 29 June 2013). Doing so would, of course, require some expertise in handling communication in and through digital media, which some articles explicitly set out to provide (e.g. explanations of PGP encryption). These articles promoted the idea that being a free and emancipated citizen had changed and that expertise in digital technologies had become a new civic duty. This claim was further supported by the current political system's failure to provide privacy protection. Thus, citizens would need to protect themselves, for example, by purchasing secure technologies. Consequently, traditional political institutions – ranging from national governments to the European Union and the European Court of Justice, and even the United Nations – were called upon to formulate 'rules for a digital society' (*FAZ*, 1 November 2013). At this point, the problem of privacy protection was connected to ongoing discussions, for instance, at the European Court of Justice's hearings on the data retention directive. While the NSA scandal posed a new problem, opinionated pieces in newspapers proposed old solutions to manage it.

Alternative voices and political actors were introduced to the media debate rather slowly. Among them, for instance, the cyberpunk movement argued early on for privacy as a basic civic right, and the hacker collective Chaos Computer Club promoted the idea of a 'data letter' (*FAZ*, 1 November 2013) that would inform users about the data being collected about them. Such references to new political actors or groups emerged more frequently only after the first shock of the NSA scandal had settled. The attention then shifted to long-term consequences and wider societal debates, in which alternative civil society organisations and technology experts encouraged citizens to broaden their knowledge about digital technologies. To remain free in a digital society, the only long-term solution seemed to be that citizens become more technology-savvy and learn to understand the political implications of digital technologies.

Overall, we can conclude that digital technologies gained more diverse meanings in the discussion by being related to both established and newly emerging political actors and institutions. At the start of the scandal, citizens were described as passive victims of surveillance, but, gradually, they were increasingly asked to actively take measures against violations of their own privacy. However, citizens were simultaneously portrayed as the wards of established political actors, who were still regarded as trustworthy enough to secure their privacy against data exploitation. The market actors were then introduced as agents to safeguard citizens' privacy by offering secure digital technologies. Alternative actors such as civil society organisations and technological experts were introduced into the debate rather slowly and mostly when discussing the broader societal and political implications of mass surveillance.

Political projections for digital technologies

The salience of different themes and their expansion and diversification offers a rough map of the sphere of legitimate controversy about NSA debate in Germany. Taking a step further, we can also analyse how broader *political projections* concerning digital technologies were debated in the opinionated sections of German quality newspapers. The call for *transformative* political action regarding the future role of digital technologies emerged only after the initial outrage following the scandalous revelations began to settle. Two main directions for future scenarios were sketched out. One argument focused on safeguarding and strengthening existing infrastructures, while the other opted for finding radically new ways of solving the problem of digital surveillance.

The argument on strengthening existing infrastructures maintained that solutions to handling digital technologies in digital societies would lie in technological pioneering, but that this must be fostered and managed by political actors within the national political systems and the EU framework. In Germany, a recurring theme in discussions about technology is the question of which ministry should regulate the internet and digital services. In the debate, the basic trust in established institutions nevertheless came with a reminder for politicians to discuss a new balance between security and freedom. Simultaneously, some voices highlighted more radical transformations of institutions. Here, both problem definitions and solutions pointed beyond the traditional political institutions.

The former editor of the *FAZ*, Frank Schirrmacher, claimed that 'we need a plan for the digital colonisation of the world' (*FAZ*, 1 November 2013) to manage the consequences of digital transformation. Schirrmacher took the tapping of Angela Merkel's mobile phone as a sign of 'a controlled and largely steered society playing a game whose rules it does not know anymore'. His conclusions were somewhere between safeguarding and reconfiguring politics. When the 'substance of future politics' is at stake, he wrote, 'unchaining the uncultivated European digital intelligence' is called for. Schirrmacher thus argued that traditional political institutions are eroding, but alternative political philosophies had not emerged yet.

Similar calls for profound political transformations and early drafts of unspecified political visions were found within other pieces. Eric Jarosinski, for one, argued that 'the internet is … *kaputt* [broken], as are our democracies' (*FAZ*, 21 January 2014). In dealing with this problem, Jarosinski stated that the NSA scandal contributed to the demystification of the internet. This enables us to ask critical questions: 'Please stay frustrated! And for God's sake: please stay disappointed', he concluded. Similarly, other authors referred to the self-healing powers of civil society. 'It is nearly utopian to ask the state to safeguard data security. The freedom of the internet was, first, sacrificed in the temple of the intelligence agencies and then choked to death by state control' (*FAZ*, 23 January 2014), one author argued.

Towards the end of the analysed period (February 2014), many commentators agreed that digital technologies profoundly challenge the realm of the political. In this debate, ideas and solutions were developed to strengthen national and European sovereignty, and some authors even tried to sketch more radical approaches. These, however, mostly remained unspecific and emphasised the role that citizens should play. There were very few moments of new, genuine political contestation. A single but influential exception was an article by Evgeny Morozov, published almost identically in both newspapers (*SZ*, 20 January 2014; *FAZ*, 24 January 2014). What makes Morozov's piece specific is that it clearly mapped out opposing scenarios in the struggle for a digital political future. One scenario was based on accepting the current status quo as the 'optimistic self-conception of the information society'. Here, the political answer to digital technologies is regulation directed through intelligence agencies or media companies. He argued that citizens actually contribute to this solution unwittingly, as they 'hand over political decisions to technocrats that might correct some details here and there, but do not profoundly question the system'. In the second scenario, 'Snowden's revelations point to the increasing and mostly ignored erosion of the democratic system.'

Morozov then went on to delineate two ways of approaching this problem. On the one hand, there are 'digital diet' approaches, which opt for reducing the presence and influence of digital technologies in everyday life. On the other hand, there are approaches that seek more radical discussions on the future of democracy. Yet readers who at this point searched for avenues for political action were left with the author's conclusion that 'we desperately need new ideas to approach this democratic deficit'. Thus, while Morozov's text was exceptional in sorting out radical approaches to dealing with the digital political future of democracies, it too stopped where contestation should begin.

A political vacuum

The NSA scandal has fed media debates about the political implications of digital technologies. Snowden's revelations demonstrated that digital technologies are being used as a means of political control, while political institutions lack effective means to regulate and control global communication flows. Against this background, we can raise the question of whether and how German quality newspapers facilitated genuine legitimate controversy about digital technologies, and whether that debate helped imagine political solutions to the problem. The notion of politicisation as provided in Europeanisation research helped us to address whether and how technology politicisation occurred in the German debate.

Our analysis sheds light on three indicators of politicisation: (1) visibility of the issue across different thematic areas; (2) its expanding reference to various political units and the diversification of arguments resulting from it; and (3) the rise and competition of projects and future projections that address *political* solutions to problems related to digital technologies.

We found that the first and second dimensions were clearly prominent in the debate. Digital technology was seen as imposing challenges not merely to the current but also future political realities. Especially, towards the end of the empirical sample, digital technologies were recognised as potential causes triggering profound transformative political processes. Based on this, we found that two strands of solutions were drafted in the course of the debate. Authors suggested strengthening existing political institutions to address the challenges that digital technologies pose for democracies, referring mostly to the nation-state or unspecified European infrastructure. Others called for more radical solutions. In these visions, citizens were assigned an important role as the driving force of democratic solutions. Yet there was a considerable absence of political projects, such as radical grass-roots democracy or the creation of global political institutions. Although a few moments in the debate hinted at political ideas and strategies, these did not result in distinguishable action plans or large-scale political mobilisation or competition.

This leads to the second question that we raised in the introduction: what kind of political action field unfolds in this debate? Despite the extensive commentary and coverage in the quality press, we argue that Snowden's revelations resulted in a political vacuum, in two regards. Political vacuum denotes relative anarchy in a situation of political transformation. In the 1950s, Karl Jaspers heavily criticised the fact that in Germany, following the fall of Hitler's totalitarian regime, democratic institutions were in place, but German citizens did not play their part as politically educated citizens: 'German democracy was not a moral and political achievement', Jaspers (1954: 596) said, 'but the symptom of a collapse [of a totalitarian system]; it was simply a way out of impotence'.

In the introduction, we suggested that politicisation implies two dimensions of the political that are closely connected to each other: moving issues into the realm of public choice, and presupposing a possibility of making collectively binding decisions. Thus, when taking into account both dimensions, the analysis of politicisation helps to specify what kind of political vacuum we might be confronted with.

Initially, it seems the first dimension is clearly met in the German case. A diverse group of voices brings to the fore that political action is called for to solve the uncertainties that stem from digital surveillance. Close up, however, the picture remains incomplete. In the wake of the transformative moment of the NSA revelations, it can be argued that the function of journalism is not only to report on cases but also to provide a *space for competing upcoming visions* about political solutions. The task of highlighting an issue and its political consequences is more traditional and familiar to journalists, and, as the German case shows, this assignment was taken seriously by quality newspapers. The task of opening a genuinely political space, though, proved to be a more difficult one.

This is not to say that political projects and projections were not developed in the German mainstream public sphere. Incidental voices of public intellectuals such as Evgeny Morozov or Constance Kurz of the Chaos Computer Club demonstrated that this option was available. However, it was not widely used. An additional pathway to new political projects was assigned for citizens, who were asked to participate in making digital political futures. Even though this function was repeatedly highlighted, citizen-related projects were hardly developed and citizens' voices not heard.

In regard to the second dimension, linking discourse to the possibility of making collectively binding decisions, the debate brought to the fore an intensified debate on *institutional disruption*. The finding that an increasing number of political institutions were being called to face these current challenges could not conceal another insight that gained importance in the course of the debate: these institutions reported lacking authority and the ability to control digital technology. This judgement pertained to the nation-state and supranational institutions, such as the EU. Against this background, it is remarkable that, from time to time, authors called for a more active citizenry and the need to invent and define a realm of the political where digital technology plays a constitutive role. What, in sum, emerges from this analysis is a debate that politicises digital technology while, at the same time, deconstructing the political framework these issues could refer to. In the debate, politicisation is directed at citizens but it fails to specify whether and how citizens are supposed to contribute to political solutions.

This lack of political projections related to an erosion of political institutions is problematic because it points, in core, to a political vacuum. All the more, this invites agents outside the political realm to assign meanings to the 'empty signifier' (Mackenzie, 2002: 25) of digital technology. Economic actors, for instance, have repeatedly noted their ambitions to replace politics by offering more 'equitable' solutions (Morozov, 2013). In February 2015, the German political magazine *Der Spiegel* ran a large piece on the political ambitions of the Silicon Valley elite. The authors claim that 'what currently happens is much more than the triumphal march of a new technology. ... It's not about the "internet" or "social networks", nor is it about secret services or Edward Snowden ... Under way is a social change that nobody will escape.' This change is driven, the authors argued, by technological elites:

> *Their worldview is designated by Libertarian radical thinkers such as Noam Chomsky, Ayn Rand and Friedrich Hayek. Taken together this makes a political philosophy that drives their action: a strange mixture of esoteric Hippie-concepts and brutal capitalism.* (Der Spiegel, 28 Feb. 2015)

While this claim can be clearly overdone, the authors convincingly show that technology elites come up with political projects and projections which could thus potentially fill the political vacuum unfolding in the media discourse on digital technology. In doing so, this piece reminds us why it is important to dive into politicisation processes as they point to transformative processes in the realm of the political.

Note

1 'Edward Snowden: the whistleblower behind the NSA surveillance revelations.' Interview published by the *Guardian*, 11 June 2013. www.theguardian. com/world/2013/jun/09/edward-snowden-nsa-whistleblower-surveillance (accessed Aug. 2016).

7

Media Diplomacy and the NSA: Making the Case at Home and Abroad for Chinese National Interests

Haiyan Wang and Ruolin Fang

The Snowden–NSA revelations drew the world superpowers and their media systems into the unfolding controversy. The revelations became one of the most important diplomatic and communication challenges the Chinese government has faced in recent years. To help manage the news, Chinese authorities orchestrated coverage of the event. Journalists at select Chinese mass-media outlets, in effect, played a double diplomatic role: they fostered a favourable image of China in the international arena and shaped understandings of national interests at home. There were three main narrative lines of the story in particular that Chinese authorities felt compelled to manage.

First, Snowden fled from Hawaii to Hong Kong as the initial location from which to publicise the leaks. In doing so, he placed himself in an ambiguous and contested zone between East and West. Despite Hong Kong's status as an international free port and a special administrative region of China, it is now Chinese territory. In his initial comments, Snowden emphasised the liberal traditions of Hong Kong. That the events were unfolding in Hong Kong and drawing attention to its 'free-port' history raised controversial issues in the Chinese domestic media landscape.

Second, Snowden made it public that China was one of the main targets of the NSA surveillance programme and that Chinese telecommunication companies, universities, and governments have been under intensive cyberattack from the United States. The Chinese government was pressed to put forward its views and propositions and, together with other governments and groups, to take up the challenge of information safety in the internet age. Ultimately, then, the event highlighted the national interests of China in the international arena.

Third, by choosing to initially hole up in Hong Kong, Snowden opened the door to accusations he might be somehow colluding with Chinese authority. These accusations were printed by many Western news outlets. The storyline spurred the Chinese government to take a defensive position and, in effect, launch a public diplomatic campaign with the help of state media.

Chinese media covered the Snowden affair abundantly. From the first-wave stories of June 2013 to February 2014, more than 40,000 stories were published by more than 800 Chinese media sources, according to the Wise News database (a major news database in China), which is an average of more than 150 stories a day. Chinese media enthusiastically participated in coverage of the global story and articulated Chinese perspectives on the revelations.

This chapter explores the complexities of the Chinese media's diplomatic role. Politicians, policy-makers and practitioners in foreign affairs have used the media for diplomatic purposes for a long time. Empirical studies regarding the practice and strategies of such a diplomacy, however, remain scarce (cf. Entman, 2008). Moreover, the media diplomacy phenomenon is often seen as targeting foreign audiences while disregarding the domestic aspects of such practices. When the state tightly controls the national media, the existence of two agendas (foreign and domestic) may be a source of legitimate controversy. The study presented in this chapter, therefore, contributes to this developing theoretical approach by looking at Chinese media diplomacy at work both nationally and internationally, and analysing the similarities and differences of these two sets of discourses. The analysis centres on journalism texts from English-language newspapers serving an international audience and Chinese outlets mostly read by a domestic audience.

To explore the Chinese government's use of media as a tool of diplomacy tied to the Snowden–NSA story, we chose four mainstream newspapers: the Chinese-language *People's Daily* and *Global Times* and the English-language *China Daily* and *Global Times*. All of the publications are officially state media in China. *People's Daily* is the national organ of the Chinese Communist Party (and regarded as 'the first paper' in China); the Chinese- and English-language editions of *Global Times*, which focus on international affairs, are subsidiaries of *People's Daily*. The Chinese-language version targets domestic readers; the English-language version targets foreign readers inside and outside the country. For years, *China Daily* has been the most widely circulated English-language newspaper in China, mainly serving international readers. With respect to the NSA events, these four newspapers became the most important and authoritative platforms for the Chinese government.

With the goal of exploring the *framing patterns* demonstrated by each newspaper, our approach combines quantitative and qualitative content analysis of their coverage. Based on the Wise News database, we searched for materials with the keywords 斯诺登 (meaning 'Snowden') for the Chinese-language newspapers and with the keywords 'Snowden' or 'NSA' for the English-language newspapers. While assessing the general volume of the Chinese coverage, the qualitative analysis mainly focuses on opinion pieces (editorials, personal commentaries, letters to the editors, etc.) in the chosen newspapers.

Defining media diplomacy

There are at least two factors that contribute to the increasing importance of media in diplomacy. One is the role of media in modern societies. During the last 150 years, communication technologies such as the telegraph, telephone, newspaper, radio, television, and now the internet have turned the media into a major factor in the organisation of social, political, economic, and cultural aspects of public life. Using the news media as a messaging tool is a fact of modern international politics. Also significant in our analysis is the shift away from secret diplomacy towards public diplomacy. Traditionally and historically, diplomacy was fairly formal, ritualised, and highly institutionalised. Operating under the principle of confidentiality and secrecy, it usually acted slowly and mainly involved government officials and diplomats (Nicolson, 1963). After World War I, however, an increasing number of politicians began to recognise the necessity of open diplomacy. In his famous post-war speech on 'The Fourteen Points', US President Woodrow Wilson called for 'open covenants of peace, openly arrived at, after which there shall be no private international understandings of any kind but diplomacy shall proceed always frankly and in the public view'.

In the same vein, a new notion of public diplomacy emerged, defined by Hans Tuch (1990: 3) as 'a government's process of *communicating with foreign publics* in an attempt to bring about understanding for a nation's ideas and ideals, its institutions and cultures, as well as its national goals and current policies'. As the former US diplomatic adviser Gifford Malone (1985: 199) puts it, public diplomacy involves 'direct communication with foreign peoples, with the aim of affecting their thinking and, ultimately, that of their governments'. The methods of conducting public diplomatic policy can be divided into at least two categories: cultural exchange, which pursues long-term gains by exporting cultural products and values to foreign publics, and media diplomacy, which focuses on real-time effects of soft power via the reporting of news and current affairs. With the advancement of media technology, various types of media have been employed in media diplomacy, and terms such as teleplomacy, photoplomacy, TV diplomacy, and so on, have gained traction.

Defined as a *communication system* (Gilboa, 2001:1) diplomacy has of course always had a close relationship with the media, but with the advancement of more intense global communication flows and networks, the subcategory *media diplomacy* has become increasingly relevant. Media diplomacy can be briefly defined as the *use of media* to elaborate and pursue diplomatic policies. Gilboa (1998: 62) defines it as 'the use of the mass media by policymakers in specific cases to send signals and apply pressure on state and non-state actors to build confidence and advance negotiations as well as to mobilize public support for agreements'.

In diplomatic history, a central role of the media as a diplomatic element can be traced back to at least the 1960s, when the governments of the United States and the Soviet Union used the media as propaganda tools targeting foreign publics, mainly by radio broadcasting during the Cold War. John F. Kennedy's televised ultimatum during the 1963 Cuban Missile Crisis epitomised this early media diplomacy. It became increasingly accentuated during the Israeli–Egyptian peace talks and the Iranian hostage crisis of the late 1970s. In a 1981 article for *Foreign Affairs*, Kenneth Adelman, who then worked for the Reagan government, even predicted that 'public diplomacy – the dissemination of America's message abroad – may become Washington's major growth industry over the coming four years' (1981: 913).

Indeed, in the 1980s, the US government made the broadcasting of Voice of America (VOA) a priority and saw it as an efficient means of exerting a direct influence on foreign publics. The official 1986 report of the US Information Agency showed that, by that time, VOA broadcasted about 1,000 hours per week in 42 languages to listeners around the world at an annual cost of between $166 million and $181 million. The emergence of CNN also played an important role in US foreign affairs. Its news coverage acted as the 'government's little helper', to use Zaller and Chiu's (1996) quip, in key foreign policy moments: the fall of communism in Eastern Europe in the 1980s, the Gulf War and Somalia War in the 1990s, and the Iraq War after the 9/11 attacks. 'The CNN effect' (Robinson, 2002; Zaller and Chiu, 1996) not only played the role of covering government decisions and military endeavours, but also helped to shape the foreign policy of the US government. In the twenty-first century, new media have stepped in to play a similarly important role. During the Obama administration, US government agencies have turned to new media platforms such as Twitter and Facebook as effective diplomatic instruments. Media diplomacy has entered the real-time and interactive era (Seib, 2012).

History suggests a central role for the United States in the development of media diplomacy. Nevertheless, many national governments, including China's, have employed similar diplomatic strategies. An early sign of this can be traced back to the Second Sino-Japanese War in the 1930s. Then, the Chinese Communist Party, or CCP, invited the American journalist Edgar Snow to the Soviet area in Yan'an for a four-month visit. The invite and Snow's visit constituted a break in China's international isolation. Snow interviewed CCP leaders, including Mao Zedong, as well as ordinary soldiers, and his stories in the UK and US media disseminated the voice of the CCP across the world for the first time. Later, the CCP invited foreign journalists from the Associated Press, Reuters, Tass, United Press International, the *New York Times, Time,* and *The Times.* From the founding of the People's Republic of China in 1949, the Chinese government has continued to use media to manage foreign affairs. It not only invites foreign journalists to cover Chinese news but also sends Chinese journalists abroad to collect information for use in shaping diplomatic strategies. In the 1950s, Mao instructed the Xinhua News Agency to send 'our journalists around the world' (Wang et al., 2013).

Since the reform policy of the 1980s – especially in recent years – the Chinese government has adopted a more aggressive use of the media in its diplomatic efforts. By 2013, the number of media outlets in foreign languages had risen to more than 200 (Yuan, 2013), and 20 TV channels targeting international audiences had been established (He et al., 2013). In 2009, China implemented the 'going out' strategy for its media, and the government invested $4 billion to support the international expansion of Chinese media. As of 2015, CCTV International has a presence in the United States, CNC International has been founded, China Radio International is broadcast in more than 60 languages, news reports from Chinese media can be seen on the billboards in Times Square in New York, and the number of foreign bureaus of the Xinhua News Agency has expanded to more than 180.

The Chinese coverage of the NSA event is best viewed in the context of the country's increasingly intensive and global media diplomacy strategy. The role of the media was central in the NSA event, because the entire story was triggered by revelations made through the media; moreover, in its aftermath, the media provided the main battlefield for state interpretations of the event.

International dialogue versus domestic harmony

Chinese press paid considerable attention to the NSA event and, on the whole, the volume of coverage was quite high. From June 2013 to February 2014, the four selected newspapers published a total of 807 news stories. *Global Times* (Chinese) carried 308 items, followed by *Global Times* (English) with 202, *China Daily* (English) with 183 and *People's Daily* (Chinese) with 114. Reporting peaked during the first three months (June–August 2013). At the beginning, the coverage focused on Snowden, his whereabouts and the global influence of the NSA-led surveillance programme. After Snowden moved to Russia, moving China out of the immediate global spotlight, the volume of coverage declined steadily. In February 2014, only 21 articles were published in the four newspapers. The trend of the gradually decreasing volume of media coverage coincides with the country's diplomatic interests. During the period when the Chinese government was most implicated in the event, the volume was high and, as the case became less urgent for the government, the volume fell.

Since Chinese media are fully controlled by the government, the volume of coverage cannot be explained by professional journalistic values only. The media cooperated closely with the government in establishing a particular foreign and domestic interpretation of the event. The volume of media coverage, the ability to manage the amount of attention given to a topic, is a key government tool in handling the complexities of international media events. The overall volume of the NSA coverage, however, says little about possible differences in foreign and domestic media-diplomacy strategies. It also does not allow for detecting where and how, if at all, the sphere of legitimate controversy emerges with regard to the event. For this, a closer look is needed.

Focusing on the role of opinion pieces in the total coverage, we can see the first signs of discrepancy – or carefully controlled diversity – in the two agendas. During the studied period, 160 opinion pieces were published in the four newspapers, which accounts for about 20% of the total coverage. The shares of opinion genres (editorials, letters to editors, commentaries) are higher in the English-language coverage. It was highest in *China Daily* (over 28%) and lowest in *People's Daily* (9.6%). The English version of *Global Times* (23%) was also more opinionated than its Chinese counterpart (16.5%). This difference tentatively indicates that a more active media diplomacy effort was directed at foreign – or internationally oriented – publics rather than at domestic publics.

The timeline trend of the opinion genres was similar to that of the overall reporting, peaking during the period June–August 2013 and gradually declining afterwards. Editorials – the official, institutional voice of the news outlets – dominated the opinion space. Among all opinion texts, 68 were editorials (42.5%) and notably 50 of them appeared in English. In Chinese-language newspapers, it was more common to represent opinions in the form of short comments. This is another distinction that demonstrates how the Chinese government uses the media to facilitate more active international public debate and prefers to minimise it on a national scale.

In addition to drawing attention to an issue through controlling the volume and the character of opinions, the media also either stimulated legitimate controversy or maintained consensus by allowing different *voices* into the coverage. Such voice management, adjusted to the needs of public diplomacy, controls the framing of media coverage.

An analysis of the 160 opinion pieces published in the four newspapers shows that the newspapers crafted the interpretation of the event by managing the diversity of authors (journalists and commentators) and news sources. Thus, while maintaining control of the debate, the coverage presented an open and all-embracing image of the nation's handling of foreign affairs and domestic discourse. The English-language newspapers understandably attached more importance to the international profile of the contributors. We found that a quarter of opinion pieces in English were contributed by foreign authors, emphasising the international character of the debate in this part of the Chinese coverage. Furthermore, the majority of these foreign authors were Americans, an indication of emphasis on the US–China relationship. In contrast, all the contributors to Chinese-language newspapers were Chinese: though they represented a variety of backgrounds, most were scholars and foreign affairs specialists.

Although quoting sources is not a common practice in opinion writing, when this happens it can reveal an author's attitude towards the subject. In the four Chinese newspapers, more than half of all opinion pieces (57.5%) included quotations of (or references to) specific sources. There were five main categories of such voices that gained access to the argumentation of opinion writers: government officials, public documents, Snowden himself, and other media and experts. Representatives of the US government and other foreign officials were the most frequently quoted. The salience of official representatives, however, again varied between the newspapers. They constituted half of the explicitly identified voices in the English-language media's opinion coverage, but only a quarter in the Chinese-language stories. Exactly the reverse situation occurred with regard to the use of media sources. Domestically oriented opinion writing quoted other media (*South China Morning Post*, the *Guardian*, the *Diplomat* and *Foreign Policy*) more frequently. It also used more references to public documents. Crucially, the domestic opinion pieces were significantly less inclined to quote Snowden. Direct quotes from Snowden appeared more frequently in the English-language material. In the coverage, expert voices were the least prominent category, which acted to mostly limit the debate within the media and political spheres.

The results show that mainstream Chinese media are generally adept at quoting various sources in order to define the event and establish the government's position. The English-language outlets' preference for quoting official sources suggests that, as a platform for international diplomacy, the externally directed media coverage was more concerned with engaging in direct dialogue with foreign governments, especially the US government. The domestic coverage, however, set the debate against the less controversial axis of other news media accounts and public documents, clearly placing priority on maintaining order rather than fostering diversity of opinions.

International relations as a frame of domestication

News media usually adopt a series of strategies to render foreign news both comprehensible to the national audience and relevant to the home nation's interest (e.g. Gurevitch et al., 1991; Cohen et al., 1996; Chan et al, 2002). With respect to the NSA event, the Chinese media's overall domestication strategy was especially evident in its selection of reported themes.

The *themes* in the opinionated stories in the Chinese newspapers can be categorised as five broad types: (1) Sino-US relations (the effect of the Snowden case on Sino-US relations and their future development); (2) international politics (the effect of the Snowden case on broader international politics, including US–Russian relations, US–European relations, and internal affairs of the United States); (3) network technology (discussions of the NSA event's implications for cybersecurity, technology, big data, multinational internet companies, and the development and future of the internet); (4) civil liberties (debates on the event's implications for the rights of privacy and freedom of speech); and (5) leak culture (commentaries on Snowden's actions and the implications of the disclosure).

Commentaries on Sino-US relations constituted the most frequent theme (38%), followed by international politics (29%) and network technology (25%). Thus, the opinion texts place a strong emphasis on international relations, framing the case as an issue between states. The initial news was about Snowden as a former contract-employee of the NSA who revealed the illegal information surveillance conducted by the country and the agency he served. This primary frame of 'the culture of whistle-blowing' and 'leaking' – suggesting a broader debate about state surveillance practices in general – could have become the main focus of the news. In the commentaries published by Chinese media, however, these were the least important themes. In contrast, issues concerning Sino-US relations, international relations, and network technology – and their close relationships with China's national interests – became more important. This way of handling the news agenda, by emphasising or downplaying different news themes in opinion pieces according to relevance to Chinese national interests, is a clear example of a domestication strategy. This strategy was a response to the NSA event and an effort to represent China's diplomatic interests in the best possible way.

Take Sino-US relations, for example. The background of this theme is clearly the change in China's diplomatic orientation and the Chinese leadership's proposition that a 'new pattern of relationship between great powers' (Zheng, 2014) should be established. This aim clearly differs from the policy of 'hiding one's capacities and biding one's time' (*taoguang yanghui*) of the 1980s and 1990s, as well as from the 'peaceful rise' policy of the first decade of the twenty-first century. The 'new power' policy, from which these differences arise, implies that China is trying to gain a new position on the international political stage. Recently, development has made China an economic power second only to the United States, a position from which it is bound to challenge the United States' long-standing economic hegemony. Therefore, addressing its relationship with the United States has become the top priority of Chinese diplomacy. The NSA event drew these two powers into the same international affair. Especially after the claims about Snowden being a Chinese spy – the 'Chinese conspiracy theory' (*zhongguo yingmou lun*) – had circulated in the international media, it is not difficult to understand why mainstream Chinese media seized this opportunity to extensively address Sino-US relations.

In the same vein, network technology is also high on the official agenda, as it is part of China's current national-development plan. The central government has explicitly advanced the aim of 'building the nation into a strong cyberpower' and recently even identified this as a key 'national strategy' (*guojia zhanlue*; Xinhua News Agency, 17 February 2014). At the international level, however, China's development of network technology has to confront US domination in the global cyberworld. As Dahong Min (22 December 2014), a Chinese expert in internet studies, puts it,

> For a long time, in the field of international internet, Western countries like the United States constantly criticise Chinese approaches to issues such as internet freedom, intellectual property, cyber attacks and commercial espionage, and in doing so dominate the rule-making and discourse on the field. (Min, 2014)

This emphasis also helps to explain why network technology was the second-most frequent theme in the materials. It could be easily framed as a sub-theme to the international relations frame. The papers did not avoid debate about technology, but they restricted it to related political implications.

In line with the interests of the Chinese government, the opinion texts on the NSA event put a great deal of emphasis on calls to rework global internet regulation. A commentary in *Global Times* (Chinese) on 21 June 2013 illustrates this emphasis:

> *The rules of regulating internet use in the world are mostly created by the Americans. The NSA 'Prism' program taught us a lesson of how deeply flawed it might be if the internet sphere was dominated by one country, the US. It is essential to strengthen international cooperation, and re-construct internet regulations through the joint efforts of international communities.*

Conversely, the discussion of civil rights was not distinctly present in the coverage. The few opinion texts that touched on this topic discussed civil rights and privacy only as they pertain to national security. For instance, a commentary in *People's Daily* on 22 January 2014 stated:

> *Cyberspace is not as good as it seems to be. It is like a reckless teenager. ... Without knowing what is happening, we leave traces of our everyday life in cyberspace, thus becoming transparent men. ... Moreover, from a larger point of view, this may well threaten national security. ... Therefore, how to build up mechanisms to protect information security is the issue facing every government in the world.*

Most commentaries avoided engaging in in-depth discussions of citizens' right to privacy and the need for oversight of government surveillance, which were in fact Snowden's core messages. Discussions of these topics are clearly a 'forbidden zone' in Chinese media. Because human rights issues have long been an important basis for the international community's criticism of China, it is unsurprising that these themes are downplayed in the Chinese media's management of the Snowden case and its diplomatic potential. The Chinese government has still not found a publicly and globally defensible and justifiable argument on these matters, a clear limitation in China's public and media diplomacy. Therefore, when an international news event involving human rights issues arose, the media typically toed the line with the government to avoid 'drawing fire' (*yinhuo shangshen*).

Discourse contestation through language choices

At the level of argumentation, Chinese media applied a series of *discourse strategies* in the interest of achieving an advantageous diplomatic position. In Fairclough's (1992) view, the essence of discourse is power. Through discourse, people engage in various social practices, shape individual subjectivity and construct power relations in the process. To capture this, in the Chinese language, the word 'discourse' is often used in the expression 'discourse power', which points to the essence of discourse as a *simultaneous mobilisation and contesting* of social power. In the NSA case, discourse contestation clearly became an important instrument of the media's diplomatic role. On the textual level, these strategies were manifested in a particular use of nouns and adjectives. On the one hand, these expressions defined the key figures in the event; on the other hand, they established a sharp contrast between the conflicting parties.

The media's characterisations of major players in the event, particularly Snowden himself, highlight these discursive choices. Across the globe, governments and journalists wrestled with the matter of how to describe Snowden. Instead of referring to Snowden as a liar, criminal, or traitor, as some US politicians tended to do, Chinese media exhibited a rather neutral and sometimes (albeit selectively) laudatory attitude towards him.

In the two English-language newspapers examined in this study, we found that the term used most frequently to describe Snowden contained the neutral word 'intelligence', as in 'intelligence worker'. 'Whistle-blower', a term drawn from Western democratic discourse, was the second most frequently used. More laudatory terms, such as 'human-rights defender', 'internet liberalist', 'liberal fighter', and even 'hero', also appeared frequently. Among all the English-language samples, only one commentary used the word 'leaker', which has a potentially negative connotation. In the two Chinese-language newspapers, however, this pro-Snowden tendency was clearly weaker, but still, a neutral and slightly commendatory attitude was evident. In these newspapers, Snowden was predominantly described using neutral terms such as 'ex-NSA employee' (*zhongqingju qian guyuan*), 'former NSA agent' (*zhongqingju qian tegong*) and '29-year-old American' (*29 sui de meiguo ren*), followed by the slightly laudatory 'whistle-blower' (*baoliao ren*). In contrast, strongly laudatory terms such as 'hero of internet freedom' (*hulianwang ziyou zhuyi yingxiong*) and 'liberty fighter' (*ziyou zhuyi doushi*) appeared only once each.

The same strategy was used to describe the US and Chinese governments. The adjectives, verbs, and nouns used to describe the US government were mostly critical and sharp: 'insincere' (*weishan*), 'utterly hypocritical' (*shifen xuwei*), 'getting into a huff' (*shua piqi*), 'thieves crying "stop thief"' (*zei han zhuo zei*), 'with concealed intentions' (*juxin poce*), 'bossy' (*yizhi qishi*), 'neither wise nor responsible' (*bu mingzhi bu fuze*), 'pretentiously' (*shayou jieshi*), 'playing politics' (*fanshou weiyun fushou weiyu*), 'using bully-boy tactics' (*shiqiang shuaheng*), 'tricks' (*baxi*), and 'disgusting' (*lingren shengyan*). Whereas some US politicians were called 'dictators' and 'big mouths' who 'spread rumours', China was described as the 'victim' (*shouhai zhe*), the 'new rising power' (*xinxing daguo*), and a 'responsible power' (*fu zeren de daguo*) that would 'take active advantage of the internet, develop scientifically, manage in accordance with the law and ensure safety'.

A commentary in *Global Times* (Chinese) on 13 July 2013 headlined 'Snowden case, America acts too shamelessly' exemplifies this trend. Almost the entire article was devoted to criticism of the US government and an exposé of its 'tricks', calling the United States a 'rogue' (*wulai*) nation. At the same time, the article portrayed China as a 'gentle, modest and courteous' power. The contrast between the two countries is taken to the extreme in the article. The beginning of the article offered the following allegation:

> According to foreign media, after the closing of the fifth round of China-US Strategic and Economic Dialogues on the 11th, US President Obama expressed 'disappointment and worry' for China on the Snowden case when meeting Chinese Vice Premier Wang Yang and State Councilor Yang Jiechi at the White House. Deputy Secretary of State William Burns repeated the word 'disappointment'. The US politicians' attitude once again proved that, on issues concerning national interest, American politicians can be quite shameless.

Next, the article referred selectively to the event, condemning the United States once again of 'unreasonable chicanery' (*wuli jiaobian*) and 'casting blame on others when they are to be blamed' (*daoda yipa*). In contrast, the Chinese government was described as always 'forbearing' (*renrang*). As the text goes:

> For some time, the Chinese government and mainstream media maintained calm and a low profile in handling the 'Snowden case', for

> which the US would be grateful according to some people. However, far
> from doing so, the US government blamed the Chinese government even
> though they were the ones to be blamed, which was really beyond the
> imagination of people who are kind-minded.

At the end of the commentary, the author once again emphasised the
contrast between the two countries, praising the 'broad mind' of the
Chinese nation while criticising the United States:

> The way US government officials handled the 'Snowden case' showed
> their usual way of talking black into white and occupying the moral high
> ground for their own benefits. However, deeply influenced by the
> Confucian culture, the Chinese people believe in 'temperate, kind,
> courteous, restrained and magnanimous diplomacy' and emphasize that
> tolerance makes greatness.

Thus, by juxtaposing China and the US, the commentary cautiously
aligned itself with Snowden's critique of the official US position on the
NSA leaks. In Chinese media diplomacy, particularly in its English-
language versions, Snowden was a 'hero' instead of a 'criminal', and his
action was not a 'crime' but a 'revelation', which exposed not only the
NSA's systematic mass surveillance but also the fact that the United
States is not a 'moral saint' but a shameless 'rogue'. Consequently, China
was represented as a frank and forthright gentleman, as opposed to a
manipulator behind the curtain. This discourse construction in accordance
with China's diplomatic interests was aimed to accumulate discourse
resources and gain more legitimacy for China's stance towards this event
through media representation.

In the light of media diplomacy, however, this discourse contestation
is, at least potentially, a double-edged sword. Although discourse can, to
some extent, be controlled for the sake of the government's diplomatic
concerns, it also has an uncontrollable aspect. In the NSA event, in order
to take advantage of the Snowden case the Chinese media were forced to
characterise him as their champion, thus at least formally aligning with
civil rights side of the controversy that broke out in the West. By doing so,
then, they too leaned temporally and discursively towards the values of
'freedom' and 'liberty', and acted as accomplices of 'whistle-blowing'.

Mobilising a criticism of 'double standards' of an ideological enemy
may have unexpected or even opposite effects. In fact, some of the Chinese

new-media platforms, like the BBS forums that are less controlled than the mainstream media, show how netizens mobilised the 'liberty' discourse – the one the government constructed about Snowden. In the BBS forums, however, users also employed it to criticise the Chinese government itself for acting exactly the opposite in its handling of domestic affairs, political dissidents, and internet policies. As a netizen wrote on Tianya Forum, one of the most popular public-affairs BBS forums in China:

> *The kind of liberty Snowden struggled for and our government praised is the kind of 'swan meat' that is unapproachable to ordinary Chinese mainland citizens like me. ... The biggest problem for us is that we don't even have the freedom to raise our voices.*

Another post on Tianya Forum reads: 'Isn't Snowden a nerd? His belief is totally distorted. "China has better press freedom and liberty of human rights than the US"? What big lies he told!'

These short examples point to an important aspect of global media events and the mediated diplomacy they mobilise. They suggest that diplomatically rational discourse contestation can be a risky game for the government to play. This is especially true in the sense that the receivers of media messages in the internet age are, more than ever before, active and autonomous individuals who tend to counter the dominant discourse imposed by the state.

Conclusion

As John B. Thompson (1995) argues, we now live in a society in which media and communication play a central role. In mediated modernity, many of our social, political, economic, and cultural activities are associated with the media. In such a context, media diplomacy has become a tool of international politics and is widely and more intensively applied by many governments, including China. Despite a rather large body of general literature on the topic, empirical studies on concrete cases of media diplomacy are scant.

In our analysis of commentaries on the NSA event published in four mainstream newspapers in China from June 2013 to February 2014, we identified four overlapping media strategies. In response to this critical international event, the Chinese government conducted media diplomacy by (1) controlling the amount of attention newspapers devoted to the controversy, (2) choosing carefully the voices and news sources included in the discussion, (3) thematically applying a strong frame of international politics, and (4) challenging the US through criticism of US 'double-standards' and representing China as a victim in the international arena.

The volume of coverage corresponded to China's diplomatic interests. In terms of managing the media's access to different voices, Chinese newspapers tried to display an image of an open and all-embracing government to both domestic and foreign publics. They published reports written by contributors with a variety of professional backgrounds and nationalities. They also quoted a variety of sources to define the event. The English-language newspapers, which target international readers, employed this strategy to a greater extent than their Chinese-language counterparts, which target a domestic audience. Regarding thematic domestication, the media's selection of frames in commentaries on the event foregrounded themes aligned with China's national interests and downplayed themes that would impair Chinese interests. With respect to discourse contestation, the media employed a series of linguistic strategies to represent China as inhabiting a morally higher position than the United States, while accusing the latter of injustice, increasing the discourse space for China in the international arena.

In sum, our study suggests that, in response to the NSA event, the Chinese state media played a clear diplomatic role. Although the emphases of the English-language and Chinese-language media differed according to their target audiences, both acted as mouthpieces for the Chinese government. On the one hand, this is certainly related to key characteristics of the Chinese media system: the media are owned by the state, controlled by the government, and serve governmental interests. This is especially the case for the four state media investigated in this study. On a more general level, however, there is not much difference between Chinese media and many Western media sources at this point in modern history. In a liberal and democratic media system, in the United States for instance, media organisations often cannot shake off their specific national imprint and end up acting – either consciously or unconsciously – as 'government's little helper' (Zaller and Chiu, 1996). In a highly mediated era, then, media diplomacy is a natural and necessary part of every government's policy. Especially in the current international order, where 'soft power' and 'hard power' are intimately interwoven (Nye, 2004), the role of media is critical.

Like any kind of public diplomacy, media diplomacy involves two-way communication. Its actors include not only the communicators but also the receivers of messages. As pointed out in the literature review, an important aspect of media diplomacy is the involvement of the public. The message the media delivers to the public according to government interests is one thing, but whether this message can gain traction with the public and whether the public will accept the message as the communicator intended is another. Accordingly, as with many other studies of international communication, a major limitation of this study is its lack of attention to the receiver of the message. If we maintain that Chinese media use various strategies, such as volume control, source management, theme domestication, and discourse contestation to serve diplomatic ends, do these strategies work? If not, why not? What inspiration can we draw for the use of media diplomacy? These questions deserve further study.

8

Governance and Digital Sovereignty: The Instrumental Role of Journalistic Consensus in Russia

Dmitry Yagodin

> *Now Snowden is in our country, and thankfully, he hasn't killed anyone. They are telling us, 'He's a criminal, hand him over'. But we don't know whether he's a criminal or not, and he hasn't committed any crimes on our territory.* (Vladimir Putin, Kremlin.ru, 4 September 2013)

In mainstream media around the world, the issues raised by the NSA scandal were not only about a threat to privacy or forms of legitimate oversight of modern intelligence. The case also provoked debate about the US technological monopoly over global information and communication networks. The large-scale exposure of US intelligence capacity bolstered a strong argument for constructing alternate model for internet governance (Bhuiyan, 2014), both globally and domestically. The Snowden debate in Russia provides an illustration of such an argument. It also highlights the role of journalism in justifying national policy.

Well before Snowden's exposés, Russia was one of the most active proponents for reforming cyberspace regulation, calling for greater control of national segments of the World Wide Web. Gradually, this view had been shaped into a rhetorical construction: the notion of *digital sovereignty*. The NSA scandal and Snowden's arrival in Russia seem to have boosted this notion in Russian minds (Soldatov and Borogan, 2015: 195–222; 2013). Understanding this particular aspect of the global response to Snowden raises the following questions. Where did the idea of *digital sovereignty* originate and how was it articulated before Snowden? What made it evolve and ripen in the media coverage of Snowden? What role did journalism play in the process?

It is impossible to understand the Russian reaction to the Snowden case without considering the pre-existing and ongoing discussion about digital sovereignty and the more general subject of internet governance. To understand the context for these discussions, we also need to grasp four overlapping issues: the role of Russia in global internet governance, the function of journalism, the value of privacy in Russia, and Russia's political stability and social order.

The criticism of global surveillance initiated by revelations about the NSA coincided broadly with revived discussions about the sovereignty of nation-states and questions of governance and control over digital communication networks situated within national borders. Theoretically, the NSA scandal presented a framework for testing the foundations of classical political realism in international relations. Famously, Hans Morgenthau (2005 [1948]) outlined the principles of political realism by claiming that, in order to understand the rationality of nation-state policies and actions, one needs to look at specific national interests rather than universal morals or even internationally agreed legal norms. Governments inevitably protect national interests by competing for various resources. Consequently, the global internet, as a crucial contemporary resource, is a prominent object of such competition.

By examining the volatile and tense Russian debate on Snowden, this chapter looks particularly at articles focusing on discussions about Snowden and internet governance in two Russian newspapers. The selected newspapers, business-oriented *Kommersant* and governmental *Rossiyskaya Gazeta* (*RG*), represent elitist and mostly state-controlled public discourse.

Journalism as policy instrument

Previous studies point to the instrumentalisation (Mancini, 2012) of the Russian mass media in the form of political clientelism (Hallin and Papathanassopoulos, 2002; Roudakova, 2008). In other words, Russian mass media directly serve the interests of their owners and sponsors. In contrast to political parallelism – where media serve the interests of competing political parties or coalitions – instrumentalisation is not aimed at such political socialisation. Instead, an instrumentalised media system furthers special interests 'that do not assume the need for and do not aim at producing active and well-informed citizens'

(Mancini, 2012: 277). Due to powerful, albeit often subtle, government interference and pressure in the editorial policies of mainstream mass media (Oates, 2007: 1294), Russian journalists could be seen as political instruments in the hands of state officials. Even when there is opportunity to resist that role, mainstream journalists tend to remain loyal toward government policies. Although Russian law prohibits censorship, the practice of self-censorship in the mass media is prevalent (Simons, 2015). Control over media content, through a carefully controlled degree of legitimate controversy, can largely be considered an official policy-making or policy-preparing tool.

Journalism everywhere domesticates news events. It perceives and represents them through the lens of national identity and looks for relevance through national interests. It does so especially when foreign news about 'them' becomes news about 'us' (Nossek, 2004). Thus, for Russian media, in principle it should have been easy to take advantage of the Snowden case and promote the strengthening of national sovereignty in cyber space. Why was Snowden not put in a role to speak about internet freedoms? Because he was hosted (and protected) by the secret services in Moscow, and was mostly spoken about and not given much time to speak out himself. In fact, Russian journalists were not able to interview Snowden during his first months in Moscow, and all his contacts with the public were carefully prepared and staged (Soldatov and Borogan 2015: 210).

This strategy effectively avoided discussions about fundamental freedoms that Snowden advocated. However, the scandal also presented a challenge to Russian authorities and journalists: how to reconcile the story of whistle-blower Snowden, his loud appreciation of privacy and individual rights, and his appeal for public oversight of surveillance with his asylum in Russia after August 2013, and the many opposing aspirations of official Russian internet governance initiatives (Nocetti, 2015). At the same time, there was the difficulty of transforming publicly announced governance policies into concrete regulatory mechanisms. It is one thing to argue for policy change at the national level, but a very different issue to challenge a dominant global model, or to convince international business and political partners that a new direction is needed.

This chapter provides evidence of media discussions aimed at domestic consumption. From the point of view of Russian journalists, at least three domestic contexts (and the related media narratives) criss-crossed in the Snowden coverage. First, for a long time, the US-led hegemony over the internet was a challenge for Russia's foreign policy as

Russia tried to preserve its international influence (Nocetti, 2015: 112). Along with other rising economic powers, such as the BRICS group, Russia attempted to develop and promote its own vision of how transnational communication networks should be regulated (Ebert and Maurer, 2013; Thussu, 2015).

Second, while eagerly building a new model of internet governance, Russia did little to counter its reputation as a country where individual freedom and privacy are not the top priority. When searching for news, Russian journalists have had more often to deal with secrecy than privacy. Exploring the general information culture in Russia, De Smaele (2007: 1310) argued that a history of strong collectivism led societal goals to 'take precedence over individual rights, such as the right to information'. Such values submitted privacy to the more familiar regime of secrecy, in which protecting the information about private lives was not considered as valuable to society as safeguarding of national secrets from private intrusion. By the mid-1990s, the Russian Federal Security Service (FSB) began officially acquiring internet surveillance tools. Later, the FSB helped develop laws requiring internet providers to cooperate with state agencies (Rohozinski et al., 2000).

Unlike the NSA's PRISM programme, the FSB surveillance system, called System for Operational-Investigative Activities (SORM), was not kept secret, and it was openly discussed in the media (e.g. *RG*, 21 October 2013). In short, SORM was a device connected to Russian internet and telephone providers' communication cables, providing the FSB with constant access to the digital traffic. Moreover, Russia's spying on its own citizens was selectively focused on dissenters and political opposition, not only digitally but physically, in a growing phenomenon termed 'watchdog surveillance' (Soldatov and Borogan, 2010: 63–4).

Third, it is crucial to bear in mind the recently unprecedented political protests that took place across Russia in 2011–12. These protests were civil society reactions to the controversial election victory of the ruling United Russia party and the return of Vladimir Putin to his third presidency. Arguably, the protests gained significant publicity and increased mobilisation through the internet, particularly via social media sites (Oates, 2013), but not mainstream journalism. This demonstrates that the state had control of almost all traditional mass media platforms, for instance, through self-censorship.

Given that its powers did not reach all digital communications, the state needed a more effective technical solution to delegate content filtering obligations to internet service providers that blocked access to blacklisted sites (Soldatov and Borogan, 2015: 166–73). This objective was motivated by the fact that the domestic protests took place concurrent with the revolutionary unrest and subsequent turmoil in Arab countries. Mistakenly or not, the Arab Spring was, in Russia, linked to two things: the capacity of Twitter to mobilise civil society, and the financial aid and information to protesters by foreign democratic governments. Whatever the true engine of the Arab Spring, Russian officials interpreted these events as a warning sign of an imminent threat to national security and began to pay close attention to social media sites and technologies on which they were based (Soldatov and Borogan, 2015: 125). Therefore, when the NSA scandal broke, it fell onto fertile ground for Russian policy-makers and their key instrument of legitimisation, the mass media. They seized on the incident to secure public consent for policy change as a response to internal political instability and dangerous external precedents.

Snowden and digital sovereignty in the media

The idea of digital sovereignty evolved from a long-standing and increasingly intensifying international discussion about the way the internet should work. Broadly taken, there are two competing approaches to internet governance: multi-stakeholderism and multilateralism (Kleinwächter and Almeida, 2015). *Multi-stakeholderism* urges the participation of a wide range of actors – governments, the private sector, civil society organisations, and technical experts – in decisions governing the internet. The main sponsors of this model have been the US and major global telecommunication corporations (also from the US). It calls for cosmopolitanism and the primacy of *post-national* borderless communication. In contrast, *multilateralism* assumes the necessity of inter*governmental* negotiations within the framework of the UN and a leading role for the International Telecommunication Union (ITU). In this model, experts and the private sector can serve as advisers to governments but not as equal partners. Russia and China have been major sponsors of this model. Their vision of international internet governance is based on a neo-Westphalian world order that respects national sovereignty in physical and cyber space (digital sovereignty).

For a detailed analysis of how these models of internet governance played out in the Russian mainstream media, we looked at all 298 stories in *Kommersant* and *Rossiyskaya Gazeta* that mention 'Snowden' from June 2013 until the end of 2015. The two newspapers made roughly similar contributions to the total sample, with 131 and 167 items respectively. There were 31 stories that mentioned 'digital sovereignty' or less frequent variants such as 'electronic', 'information', 'internet', or 'network sovereignty'. For convenience, these other variants are referred to as digital sovereignty throughout the analysis, unless the wording is relevant for their specific role in shaping the debate. As noted above, though, the narrative of digital sovereignty is a longer one. Thus, the search for stories on 'digital sovereignty' was extended to a period before Snowden's revelations to offer a background and comparison. Notably, 'digital sovereignty' appeared during 2004 in stories discussing internet development in Belarus, and in 2011 concerning China and Vietnam – but never before 2012 in relation to Russia itself.

From June 2013 to the end of that year, both newspapers of course published scores of stories about Snowden, altogether 186 items, averaging 26 items a month and peaking at 57 items in July. At the same time, however, only one story mentioned digital sovereignty, suggesting the two debates were running separately. One year after the Snowden incident, the Russian media discussion of digital sovereignty evolved rapidly. The number of digital sovereignty items grew. During the second half of 2015, it reached numbers similar to the Snowden discussion of 2013.

In this chapter, I will take a detailed look at some newspaper stories where the concept of digital sovereignty was launched and discussed, aiming to highlight how the Snowden incident intensified the efforts in by Russian authorities to shape the concept into a key notion of official policy. By focusing on particular stories and actual moments of articulations we get a sense of the landscape in which the NSA affair took place in Russia and the ways in which the sphere of legitimate controversy – and the contradictory and even paradoxical meanings activated by Snowden (in Russia) – were managed.

During the pre-Snowden period, two moments of media attention to digital sovereignty are worthy of note: the early foreign references (three items) and the first domestic application of the term (two items). This is the period of sporadic and non-systematic articulation of 'digital' with 'sovereignty'. The term was still being shaped.

The post-Snowden period, though much richer, is more problematic to pin down. One obvious step is to determine when both subjects were discussed simultaneously or even in relation to one another. The beginning of 2014 witnessed the moment of confluence, when 'Snowden' and 'digital sovereignty' appeared in the same news items. Before that, despite the thematic closeness of the subjects, the newspapers did not discuss them together. Therefore, the two stories on digital sovereignty in February 2014 are counted in the seven Snowden articles. The stories are both from *RG* (17–18 February 2014). Because such an explicit overlap does not occur at any other time in 2013–15, they present another crucial point for textual analysis.

The early examples of content control

In Russia, the first reference to digital sovereignty was made among IT security specialists. Igor Ashmanov, a well-known internet technology developer and business person, is credited as the founder of the concept, which he promoted at the 2013 iForum in Kyiv, Ukraine. Russian lawmakers picked up on his ideas and adapted the notion to the political language of parliamentary work. These ideas developed while Russia's political isolation was growing and the Russian media was engaged in contests with the West. As Emily Parker (2014) has explained, the increased regulation of digital communication was a symptom of the Russian political elite's, and in particular Putin's, 'cyberphobia'.

Long before the idea of digital sovereignty entered the domestic Russian public discourse, similar concepts surfaced in foreign news sections. In 2004, in neighbouring Belarus, authorities used 'information sovereignty' to explain temporary shutdowns of Russian television channels, blocking particular programmes or moving them out of prime-time slots (*Kommersant*, 19 April 2004). In Belarus, a former Soviet republic with a predominantly Russian-speaking population, local television stations coexisted with channels from Moscow. Thus when tensions arose between the two countries, the local audience received conflicting agendas. It was, therefore, politically expedient that Belarus, as a sovereign (authoritarian) state, pursued stronger control over the media.

Another milestone of the evolving media discussion of digital sovereignty occurred in 2011, when Ashmanov's company worked in Vietnam, helping the country to develop a national search engine to counter Google's dominance. *Kommersant* coverage of this story

153

highlighted Russians working for the Vietnamese government, to which they had been 'actively selling the idea of "electronic sovereignty" and a national search engine service as one of its components' (*Kommersant*, 6 June 2011). The article also explained that the project was a platform for openly rivalling Google in other East Asian countries. It stated that the foreign contract was part of a longer cooperation between the Russian IT company and Vietnam. Earlier, Ashmanov had already helped build infrastructure for internet-traffic filtering in Vietnam.

Later the same year, the Shanghai Cooperation Organisation (SCO) held its annual summit in Astana, Kazakhstan. The *Kommersant* reporter quoted Kazakh President Nursultan Nazarbayev:

> *It is time to introduce new concepts into international law – 'electronic borders' and 'electronic sovereignty'. We need to support the important work of our Russian and Chinese friends and to develop a common position on this issue. We have to consider the creation of a special body within the SCO, to perform the functions of cyber-pol.* (*Kommersant*, 16 June 2011)

The reporter described this task as too ambitious yet potentially attractive for SCO leaders 'given the destructive influence the internet has had in toppling the authoritarian regimes in North Africa'. According to the story, the Russian delegation reacted positively to the initiative. Then the narrative shifted from examples of failed electronic sovereignty (Libya and Egypt) to the successful Chinese model, praised for its 'powerful filtering system' and the role that '30,000 members of cyber police play to support it'.

These early examples of 'digital sovereignty' are few and scattered, but they shed light on the climate that preceded the exponential growth in the Russian media of debate on the theme. Thematically, the argument was already emerging clearly, defining sovereignty as control over politically and symbolically relevant content. Meanwhile, the countries that appeared in this early coverage – Belarus, Vietnam and China – are typical objects of studies measuring the filtering of internet content across the globe (Deibert, 2009). Despite numerous associations with undemocratic regimes, the coverage points out that controlling internet content, either through filtering entire sites or through adjusting search results, threatens many countries, including Russia.

Plans for Russia's cyber security strategy

At the end of 2012, following the surges of political protest that followed the controversial elections of the state Duma and President Putin, Russian authorities established the Commission on Information Society Development as part of the upper house of the Russian parliament. It was a temporary organisation with one central task: to prepare new information and communication legislation. The commission was given a three-year deadline (2016) to propose Russia's cyber security strategy. The forthcoming document would supersede already outdated information-security strategy from the year 2000.

The work of the commission was directly connected to the formal introduction of digital sovereignty into the Russian political discourse. *Kommersant* described the initiative in an article headlined 'The Council of the Federation attends to digital sovereignty: Cyber security strategy has been outlined' (*Kommersant,* 6 November 2012). The story included the Head of the Commission, Senator Ruslan Gattarov, stating that the goal of the new cyber-security strategy was digital sovereignty for Russia. The Senator explained that information threats, which targeted individual citizens, business interests, and the state, justified changes in governance.

Kommersant cited threats listed in the Commission documents as follows: *Ordinary people* could be affected by the collection and leakage of private information, fraud, and dissemination of dangerous content. *Business* would suffer from poorly protected e-banking services and online trade disruptions. For example, Gattarov compared Google's email service Gmail and its Russian analogue Yandex Mail, saying that the foreign email service could not guarantee full secrecy of correspondence and potentially allowed spying. The independent national alternative was purportedly accountable, at least to the Russian authorities. This link to state security corresponded to the third category of threats: those targeting *institutions of the state* (e-government, bureaucratic communications, and national foreign trade).

As described in the story, enhanced security did not require autonomy over domestic hardware and software. Russian regulators needed only to access the source code of the borrowed technologies. *Kommersant* explained that Gmail and Skype were potential national security threats because the authorities could not quickly decrypt the messages, and because the services were 'used by extremists and other groups'. This came close to saying that the Russian secret services were eager to intercept all digital communication to protect citizens, business, and the state from vaguely defined threats ('other groups'). The story ended by stating that the Commission was only one part – at least the most public portion – of several platforms meant to prepare and implement cyber security strategy.

Another publicly discussed part of Russian cyber policy was the launch of a special agency within the Foreign Ministry to tackle international information security. As another *Kommersant* story (25 January 2013) explained, the main purpose of the new agency was to promote a code of conduct and improve trust in the internet. The article begins by stating that, since 2011, 'the internet and questions of information security became one of the priorities in Moscow's internal and foreign politics'. As the reporter clarified, the underlying reason for this change was an attempt to use the UN and OSCE to convince the international community that national sovereignty and non-intervention applied to internet governance and cyber communication.

The main argument that the reporter picked up from the official documents was based on three rhetorical elements. First, according to Russian authorities, 'almost all leading countries' regulated the internet. Second, the most active suppression of internet freedom – blocking and filtering of content – occurred in the US. Finally, six months before Snowden, Russian experts in the Ministry of Foreign Affairs informed the public that US intelligence services monitored private communications between foreigners and Americans.

The paradox of these two news stories – and the discourse they articulate – is that they present digital sovereignty as a foundation for national security, not only internationally but also domestically. Both argue for protecting Russia's digital space from outside intervention and internal political resistance. By claiming the right of special agencies to monitor and filter internet communication, this discourse ignored complaints about the invasion of Russian citizens' privacy. The only concern was that the tools of potential invasion were in the wrong hands. Early media interest in the subject was found only in *Kommersant*, whereas the government-led *Rossiyskaya Gazeta* turned its attention to the subject only after the Snowden revelations, which may indicate the importance that the scandal had among Russia's political elites.

Did Snowden really matter?

Several theoretical arguments explain the urgency of reforming internet governance. These include the assertion that the expanding internet connects more people from the highly populated developing countries, making it less Western and less homogeneous. From a critical perspective, the multi-stakeholder internet governance, despite its democratic and cosmopolitan overtones, can be seen as hegemonic, a smokescreen that covers privileged Western dominance of the existing order (Carr, 2015). Even though Western-led globalisation increasingly penetrates all spheres of life, it has been met with some resistance. Weiss and Wilkinson (2014: 213) noted that 'everything is globalised – that is, everything except politics'. Thus, one should not exaggerate Snowden's role in hastening internet governance and discussion of digital sovereignty among observers who have criticised the existing order.

The early development of the internet was accompanied by a cultural paradigm that proclaimed borderless and decentred cyberspace as a global commons (Turner, 2006; Benkler, 2006). However, this was mostly a normative conviction about what the internet *should* be, rather than a description that would have taken security and infrastructure into account (Lewis, 2010: 56). In the paradigm promoted by internet pioneers, national cybersecurity was either downplayed, ignored, or unheard of, perhaps because of US technological dominance, or due to the vision reflected: 'Western political values, such as openness for ideas and discourse' (ibid., 63). These are, Lewis reminds us, 'not universally esteemed by all governments'.

Meanwhile, governments began to crave digital sovereignty the same way that they enjoyed physical sovereignty (Nocetti, 2015: 111). Russia, as successor to the Soviet Union, was a relatively new state in the sense that it was adapting to new geopolitical realities and may have been more sensitive about its sovereignty than older states with strong cosmopolitan trends (ibid., 129). Therefore, it should not be surprising to find that Russian newspapers rarely discussed Snowden and digital sovereignty in the same breath – as mentioned above, in the empirical analysis these subjects appeared together only twice. Nonetheless, this disconnection does raise questions.

Was the disjunction due to some unspoken, Russian journalistic principle of not linking the sacrifice of an individual life to far-reaching policy consequences? After all, we know how uncomfortable any reference to grass-roots resentment or successful dissent may be for the Russian political agenda. Or was it because of conscious belief that stronger digital sovereignty was justified? Looking at the two moments when the topics touched each other may pinpoint how the subjects were related.

Snowden and the future of the internet were explicitly connected in a *Rossiyskaya Gazeta* interview with Andrei Kolesnikov, director of the national coordination centre of internet domains (*RG*, 17 February 2014). This interview highlights key moments in the sphere of legitimate controversy in Russia by showing how different meanings are controlled. The journalist formulated a question with a vague, unidentifiable subject: '*People* say that the Snowden story has changed the world. What about the internet? Will the control over information dissemination become tighter?' (emphasis added). The expert's answer emphasised how the Snowden story brought discussion about digital sovereignty to the public domain in a positive way. Kolesnikov lamented Russia's overdependence on foreign hardware and software, defining digital sovereignty as *technological domestication* with preference and incentives for Russian-produced IT-ware through 'at least restricting the use of foreign software in critically important industries'.

In the interview, he was less concerned about privacy, pointing out that ordinary people consciously exchanged it for convenience of communication. Moreover, Kolesnikov was quoted as saying that 'in a globalised and transparent world, however strange it may appear, people and countries need to get used to living without secrets'. According to him, content filtering was more important for sovereignty. He argued: 'alas, the internet is already different in different countries, the nice utopia about universal net equality has failed', suggesting that international regulation of technological specifications was necessary because it would enable filtering without disconnecting segments of the internet. Thus, the justification of digital sovereignty in this piece rested on Snowden as evidence for promoting a transition from foreign to domestically produced and licensed infrastructure that would facilitate the national IT industry while providing more governmental control.

The expert opinion described above relies on two sets of arguments – recognising the value of individual rights stretching across borders and collective well-being within socio-political limits of nation-states. Sovereignty appears as a conscious choice between a seemingly utopian notion of privacy that is so easily traded by the people themselves and pragmatic alignment with national economic (if not political) interests.

We should favour digital sovereignty, as it may benefit us as individuals indirectly through a stronger national digital economy. At the same time, the argument goes, we should also get used to the fact that privacy is a matter of consumer habits and voluntarily decisions.

In the next issue of *Rossiyskaya Gazeta* (18 February 2014) another news story described Snowden as causing a new trend: de-globalisation of the internet. The journalist wrote:

> *The internet, usually understood as a global phenomenon, could actually at some point become a thing of the past. In its place will be dozens of completely autonomous national networks with limited access to foreign sources. Until recently, such a closed network existed only in China, with its famous 'great firewall'. However, today a number of countries, including, by the way, Russia, have already adopted or considered laws that prohibit the use of foreign services in some cases. Given the continuous growth and increasing complexity of threats, such aspirations will grow like a snowball.*

Such journalistic reflection helps to accustom the public to upcoming changes. Discussing the future of the internet, the article refers to China's example with adjectives like 'famous' and 'great', evoking positive connotations. Furthermore, Russian internet governance was not exclusively Russian; it was said to be part of a general, international movement. Restrictions on the internet were also presented as a normal reaction to all kinds of cyber threats. As the other part of this story suggested, it was imperative that all the practical steps in reforming internet governance were performed outside US control. This claim was, of course, a more convincing position after the NSA scandal.

Although the coverage of Snowden and digital sovereignty directly overlapped very little, in the broader flow of public discourse, there were more indirect links than these two stories. Indeed, what was the Snowden coverage about, if not digital sovereignty and internet governance? After the first media reaction to Snowden, both newspapers presented a variety of themes and arguments distantly related to internet governance. This included comparison between the current unipolar world order (described as flawed and dangerous) and a potential multipolar world (construed as more balanced and safer). The contrast between US global dominance and the regimes in Latin America, Asia, and Eurasia made Snowden a heavy rhetorical weapon.

Much of the Russian coverage about Snowden and the NSA also referred to the scandal as a crisis of the existing world order, which indirectly served as criticism of the multi-stakeholder internet governance model. In particular, *RG* emphasised the NSA scandal as the effect of geopolitical 'unipolarity' that should be countered by the 'multipolar system of international relations'. In one commentary, Karen Brutents (*RG*, 4 April 2014), a seasoned political analyst and former Soviet apparatchik from the Central Committee of the Communist Party, wrote:

> *Casual wiretapping of Europeans, including their leaders, the rude pressure in connection with the Snowden case, and, in defiance of all norms, the barring of European airspace for the Bolivian President, represents, I think, a direct attack on the dignity and self-esteem of the Europeans.*

Looking at the broader trend of discourse related to Snowden, one should also bear in mind that, at the beginning of 2014, Russia became involved in the military conflict in Eastern Ukraine. The subsequent Western sanctions aggravated Russia's international relations and added new *instrumental* tasks for the Russian mass media. The anti-Western rhetoric primarily targeted the domestic audience. Closely related to that, the ongoing cyberwar and general resentment of the West (mainly the US) on that front were prominent. A large part of the Snowden coverage touched upon US accusations of cyber-espionage against China. The NSA scandal was clearly used to dilute or even reverse these claims.

The coverage on Snowden and digital sovereignty paid little attention to the interests of civil society or the private sector. Very few business representatives were interviewed regarding their views on the internet. When they were given a voice in newspapers, these interviewees introduced moments of legitimate controversy into the debate. For example, in a story that combines Snowden and digital sovereignty issues (*RG*, 18 February 2014), Aleksandr Gostev from Kaspersky Lab, a global software security firm, argued against the dominant rhetoric. He said that alternative channels of communication that allow bypassing existing internet traffic routes were only possible through commercial initiatives. This implies internet governance by the multi-stakeholderism model. His point is that governments would not be able to work on such projects alone. Thus, the state policy of promoting the multilateralism of internet governance was challenged. However, as previously noted, such controversial moments were exceptions.

Overall, the evidence from Russia is that mainstream journalism stayed within a consensus about digital sovereignty leading to a particular model of internet governance. In both samples, the newspapers relied on statements made by politicians and technical advisers to policy-makers. When a politician is quoted saying 'our children get lost in the global web' (*RG*, 25 October 2013), the angle prepares readers for proposals on tighter regulation in the name of protecting family values. This story exemplifies the sort of argument that began by raising a fearful issue ('protecting our children'). It then touches briefly on Snowden's exposé of the US spy programme, and ends with a paragraph stating that the Parliament had approved new laws on personal data protection. In such articles, references to Snowden were neither central nor decisive. Rather, their role was secondary and supportive.

As a continuation of this argument, in the media articles analysed, there was often a distinction between individual rights and the interests of society. Technical experts were mobilised to explain how content is filtered virtually everywhere in the world, and how citizens voluntarily exchange their privacy for the convenience of digital services. Eventually, the argument closed with a suggested solution: digital sovereignty of infrastructure, and communication technology that would enable control of content.

Conclusion

In July 2014, a year after Snowden's revelations, at the 6th BRICS Summit in Brazil, delegates discussed a new model for the internet. In this initiative – as a solution reducing the dependency of emerging economies on US-controlled communication infrastructure – access to the internet would bypass the existing routes and digital protocols. In the EU, parallel discussions were reactivated after the NSA scandal, though with differently articulated purposes. In the broad context of these discussions, Russia, as part of BRICS and a crucial communication hub between Europe and Asia, was also a key voice in the evolving Snowden–NSA scandal.

The irony of Snowden's situation was that he received political asylum as a defender of free thought in a country rated very low for human rights and freedom of speech (e.g., Soldatov and Borogan, 2015). The Russian media show that public discourse often took spying for granted, but insisted that spying must be fair; that is, available to other countries as an effective means of gathering counter-intelligence. The way the Russian news media articulated questions of internet governance can be seen both as countering US hegemony and as legitimising a further tightening of the internet and narrowing media freedom at the national level. In the journalistic interpretation, the consolidation of opinions around the idea of digital sovereignty, the protection of national communication from 'external intrusion', distracted the public from growing domestic tension and from potential social and political unrest.

Public discourse in Russia tended to describe the NSA scandal as the result of geopolitical 'monopolarity' that should be countered by the 'multipolar system of international relations'. This corresponded to the multilateral system of internet governance promoted by Russia. The coverage in Russia prioritised arguments for stronger digital sovereignty. By emphasising the subject, the media converted the definition of cyber security from protection against surveillance malware to the control of internet access on Russian territory. Whereas the former was merely a technical problem, the latter was presented as a serious obstacle to national stability, needing urgent legislation.

The media coverage analysed here shows how challenges to national security and sovereignty increasingly overlap with obstacles to political order and legitimacy. These concerns have been reflected in the 2016 version of Russian information security strategy.[1] This suggests a need for continued, in-depth research, and a comparison of the public discussion between 2012 and 2015 with the resulting policy.

This chapter has mostly focused on the mainstream media. It takes, however, one step outside this *instrumental* journalism to encounter more controversial and deviating coverage, for example, in the writing of marginalised critics of Russia's own surveillance state. Investigative journalist Andrei Soldatov's column for the English-language *Moscow Times* (18 June 2013) was headlined 'NSA is no match for the FSB'. He pointed to even less accountability on the part of the FSB for how it intercepts communication. The same eavesdropping equipment that the FSB uses, by law, to connect to Russian service providers was exported to the territories of the former Soviet Union. Soldatov challenged the legitimacy of the dominant view, but could have hardly threatened the mainstream media's consensus on digital sovereignty.

Rephrasing the headline, one may say Soldatov's piece was 'no match' for the prime-time televised talk between Snowden and Putin in April 2014. When approached by Snowden with a pre-recorded question about Russia's surveillance programme, Putin famously replied 'You are a former secret agent. I used to work for an intelligence agency, so we are going to talk the same professional language' (1TV, 17 Apr 2014). What many journalists around the world did not mention was the reaction of the studio audience. When Putin paused shortly after the first sentence, then slowly, as if hesitating, continued about his own background, the crowd burst into wild applause.

Note

1 See *Doctrine of Information Security for the Russian Federation* (2016), Doktrina informatsionnoi bezopasnosti Rossiyskoi Federatsii. Available at *Rossiyskaya Gazeta*, 6 December, https://rg.ru/2016/12/06/doktrina-infobezobasnost-site-dok.html (accessed Feb. 2017).

References

Abbott, Andrew (1988). *The System of Professions: An Essay on the Division of Expert Labor.* Chicago: Chicago University Press.

Adelman, K. (1981). Speaking of America: Public Diplomacy in our Time. *Foreign Affairs* 59(4), 913–16.

Altheide, D. L., and Snow, R. P. (1979). *Media Logic.* London: SAGE.

Anderson, C. W., Bell, E., and Shirky, C. (2013). *Post-Industrial Journalism: Adapting to the Present.* New York: Tow Center of Digital Journalism.

Anderson, D. (2015). *A Question of Trust: Report of the Investigatory Powers Review.* https://terrorismlegislationreviewer.independent.gov.uk/wp-content/uploads/2015/06/IPR-Report-Print-Version.pdf (accessed May 2016).

Andrejevic, M. (2013). *Infoglut: How Too Much Information is Changing the Way We Think and Know.* New York: Routledge.

Balleste, R. (2015). *Internet Governance: Origins, Current Issues, and Future Possibilities.* Lanham, MD: Rowman & Littlefield.

Bauman, Z., Bigo, D., Esteves, P., Guild, E., Jabri, V., Lyon, D., and Walker, R. B. J. (2014). After Snowden: Rethinking the Impact of Surveillance. *International Political Sociology* 8(2), 121–44.

Baume, S., and Papadopoulos, Y. (2015). Transparency: From Bentham's Inventory of Virtuous Effects to Contemporary Evidence-Based Scepticism. *Critical Review of International Social and Political Philosophy.* http://dx.doi.org/10.10 80/13698230.2015.1092656.

Beck, U. (2006). *Cosmopolitan Vision.* Cambridge: Polity.

Bell, E. (2016). Snowden Interview: Why the Media isn't Doing its Job. *Columbia Journalism Review,* 10 May. http://www.cjr.org/q_and_a/snowden. php (accessed Aug. 2016).

Benkler, Y. (2006). *The Wealth of Networks: How Social Production Transforms Markets and Freedom.* New Haven: Yale University Press.

———. (2011). A Free Irresponsible Press: Wikileaks and the Battle over the Soul of the Networked Fourth Estate. *Harvard Civil Rights-Civil Liberties Law Review* 46, 311–97. http://nrs.harvard.edu/urn-3:HUL.InstRepos:10900863 (accessed Feb. 2016).

Benkler, Y., Roberts, H., Faris, R., Solow-Niederman A., and Etling, B. (2013). *SOPA/PIPA Study Social Mobilization and the Networked Public Sphere: Mapping the SOPA-PIPA Debate*. Cambridge, MA: Berkman Center for Internet and Society at Harvard University Publication Series. http://cyber.law.harvard. edu/publications/2013/social_mobilization_and_the_networked_public_ sphere (accessed Feb. 2016).

Bennett, W. L. (1990). Toward a Theory of Press–State Relations in the United States. *Journal of Communication* 40(2), 103–25.

Benson, R., and Neveu, E. (eds) (2005). *Bourdieu and the Journalistic Field*. Cambridge: Polity.

Berglez, P. (2008). *Global Journalism: Theory and Practice*. New York: Peter Lang.

Best, K. (2010). Living in the Control Society: Surveillance, Users and Digital Screen Technologies. *International Journal of Cultural Studies* 13(1): 5–24.

Bhuiyan, A. (2014). *Internet Governance and the Global South: Demand for a New Framework*. London: Palgrave Macmillan.

Birchall, C. (2016). Digital Age: Managing Secrecy. *International Journal of Communication* 10, 152–63.

Blondiaux, L. (1998). *La fabrique de l'opinion*. Paris: Le Seuil.

Boltanski, L., and Thévenot, L. (2006). *On Justification: Economies of Worth*. Princeton: Princeton University Press.

Bourdieu, P. (1973). L'opinion publique n'existe pas. *Les Temps Modernes* 318, 1292–1309.

———. (1993). *The Field of Cultural Production*. Cambridge: Polity.

Braithwaite, J., and Drahos, P. (2000). *Global Business Regulation*. Cambridge: Cambridge University Press.

Brandeis, L. (1914). *Other People's Money*. Louisville, KY: Louis D. Brandeis School of Law Library, Brandeis School of Law. https://louisville.edu/law/library/ special-collections/the-louis-d.-brandeis-collection/other-peoples-money-by- louis-d.-brandeis (accessed Feb. 2016).

Buzan, B., Wæver, O., and de Wilde, J. (1998). *Security: A New Framework for Analysis*. Boulder, CO, and London: Lynne Rienner Publishers.

Carlson, M., and Lewis, S. (2015). *Boundaries of Journalism: Professionalism, Practices and Participation*. New York: Routledge.

Carr, M. (2015). Power Plays in Global Internet Governance Millennium. *Journal of International Studies* 43, 640–59.

Chadwick, A. (2013). *The Hybrid Media System: Politics and Power*. Oxford: Oxford University Press.

Chadwick, A., and Collister, S. (2014). Boundary-Drawing Power and the Renewal of Professional News Organizations: The Case of the *Guardian* and the Edward Snowden NSA Leak. *International Journal of Communication* 8(22), 2420–41.

Chan, M., Lee, C., Pan, Z., and So, C. (2002). Domesticating International News: A Comparative Study of the Coverage on the Hong Kong Handover. *Mass Communication Research* 72, 1–28 [in Chinese].

Christensen, L., and Cheney, G. (2015). Peering into Transparency: Challenging Ideals, Proxies, and Organizational Practices. *Communication Theory* 25(1), 70–90.

Clausen, L. (2003). *Global News Production*. Copenhagen: Copenhagen Business School Press.

———. (2004). Localizing the Global: 'Domestication' Processes in International News Production. *Media, Culture and Society* 26(1), 25–44.

Cohen, A., Levy, M. R., Roeh, I., and Gurevitch, M. (1996). *Global Newsroom, Local Audiences: A Study of the Eurovision News Exchange*. London: John Libbey.

Coleman, G. (2014). *Hacker, Hoaxer, Whistleblower, Spy: The Many Faces of Anonymous*. New York: Verso.

Couldry, N. (2003). *Media Rituals: A Critical Approach*. London: Routledge.

———. (2012). *Media, Society, World: Social Theory and Digital Practice*. Cambridge: Polity.

Couldry, N. and Hepp, A. (2017). *The Mediated Construction of Reality*. Cambridge: Polity.

Darnton, R. (2011). *The Devil in the Holy Water, or the Art of Slander from Louis XIV to Napoleon*. Philadelphia: University of Pennsylvania Press.

Davet, G., and Lhomme, F. (2011). *Sarko m'a tuer*. Paris: Stock.

Dayan, D., and Katz, E. (1992). *Media Events*. Cambridge, MA: Harvard University Press.

De Smaele, H. (2007). Mass Media and the Information Climate in Russia. *Europe-Asia Studies* 59(8), 1299–1313.

De Wilde, P., and Zürn, M. (2012). Can the Politicization of European Integration be Reversed? *Journal of Common Market Studies* 50(1), 137–55.

Deibert, R. (2009). The Geopolitics of Internet Control: Censorship, Sovereignty, and Cyberspace. In: A. Chadwick and P. Howard (eds), *Routledge Handbook of Internet Politics*. London: Routledge, 323–36.

Dijck, J. van, and Poell, T. (2013). Understanding Social Media Logic. *Media and Communication* 1(1), 2–14.

Donsbach, W., and Patterson, T. (2004). Political News Journalists: Partisanship, Professionalism, and Political Roles in Five Countries. In: F. Esser and B. Pfetsch (eds), *Comparing Political Communication: Theories, Cases, and Challenges*. Cambridge: Cambridge University Press, 251–70.

Downie, L. (2013). *The Obama Administration and the Press*. New York: Committee to Protect Journalists. https://cpj.org/reports/us2013-english.pdf (accessed May 2016).

Ebert, H., and Maurer, T. (2013) Contested Cyberspace and Rising Powers. *Third World Quarterly* 34(6), 1054–74.

Entman, R. (2008). Theorizing Mediated Public Diplomacy: The U.S. Case. *International Journal of Press/Politics* 13(2), 87–102.

Ericson, R., Baranek, P., and Chan, J. (1989). *Negotiating Control: A Study of News Sources*. Toronto: Toronto University Press.

Esser, F., and Umbricht, A. (2013). Competing Models of Journalism? Political Affairs Coverage in US, British, German, Swiss, French and Italian Newspapers. *Journalism* 14(8), 989–1007.

Ettema, J. S. & Glasser, T. L. (1998). *Custodians of Conscience: Investigative Journalism and Public Virtue*. New York: Columbia University Press.

Fairclough, N. (1992). *Discourse and Social Change*. Cambridge: Polity Press.

Farge, A. (1986). *La vie fragile: Violence, pouvoirs et solidarités à Paris au XVIIIe siècle*. Paris: Hachette.

———. (1992). *Dire et mal dire: L'opinion publique au XVIIe siècle*. Paris: Le Seuil.

Fidler, D. (2015). *The Snowden Reader*. Bloomington, IN: Indiana University Press.

Fisher, Eran (2010). Contemporary Technology Discourse and the Legitimation of Capitalism. *European Journal of Social Theory* 13(2), 229–52.

Flyverbom, M. (2016). Transparency: Mediation and the Management of Visibilities. *International Journal of Communication* 10, 110–22.

Flyverbom, M., Leonardi, P., Stohl, C., and Stohl, M. (2016). The Management of Visibilities in the Digital Age: Introduction. *International Journal of Communication* 10, 98–109.

Fox, J. (2007). The Uncertain Relationship between Transparency and Accountability. *Development in Practice* 17(4–5), 663–71.

Fraser, N. (2014). *Transnationalizing the Public Sphere*. Cambridge: Polity.

Galtung, J., and Ruge-Holmboe, M. (1965). The Structure of Foreign News. *Journal of Peace Research* 2(1), 64–91.

Ganesh, S. (2016). Managing Surveillance: Surveillant Individualism in an Era of Relentless Visibility. *International Journal of Communication* 10, 164–77.

Garsten, C., and de Montoya, M. (eds) (2008). *Transparency in a New Global Order: Unveiling Organizational Visions*. Cheltenham: Edward Elgar Publishing.

Garton Ash, T. (2016). *Free Speech: Ten Principles for a Connected World*. New Haven: Yale University Press.

Gieryn, T. (1983). Boundary-Work and the Demarcation of Science from Non-Science: Strains and Interests in Professional Ideologies of Scientists. *American Sociological Review* 48(6), 781–95.

Gilboa, E. (1998). Media Diplomacy: Conceptual Divergence and Application. *Harvard International Journal of Press/Politics* 3(3), 56–75.

———. (2001). Diplomacy in the Media Age: Three Models of Uses and Effects. *Diplomacy and Statecraft* 12(2), 1–28.

Gill, P. (2012). *Policing Politics: Security Intelligence and the Liberal Democratic State*. New York: Routledge.

Greenwald, G. (2014). *No Place to Hide: Edward Snowden, the NSA and the Surveillance State*. London: Penguin.

Gurevitch, M., Levy, M., and Roeh, I. (1991). The Global Newsroom: Convergences and Diversities in the Globalisation of Television News. In: P. Dahlgren and C. Sparks (eds), *Communications and Citizenship: Journalism and the Public Sphere in the New Media Age*. London: Routledge, 195–216.

Gurnow, M. (2014). *The Edward Snowden Affair: Exposing the Politics and Media behind the NSA Scandal*. Indianapolis: Blue River Press.

Gürses, S., Kundnani, A., and van Hoboken, J. (2016). Crypto and Empire: The Contradictions of Counter-Surveillance and Advocacy. *Media, Culture and Society* 38(4), 576–90.

Hallin, D. (1986). *The Uncensored War*. Berkeley, CA: Berkeley University Press.

———. (1992). The Passing of High Modernism of American Journalism. *Journal of Communication* 42(3), 14–25.

———. (1994). *We Keep America on Top of the World: Television Journalism and the Public Sphere*. Abingdon: Routledge.

Hallin, D., and Mancini, P. (2004). *Comparing Media Systems: Three Models of Media and Politics*. New York: Cambridge University Press.

Hallin, D., and Pathanassopoulos, S. (2002). Political Clientelism and the Media: Southern Europe and Latin America in Comparative Perspective. *Media, Culture and Society* 24, 175–95.

Harding, L. (2014). *The Snowden Files: The Inside Story of the World's Most Wanted Man*. London: Guardian Books.

Hartley, J. (2011). *Communication, Cultural and Media Studies: The Key Concepts*. New York: Routledge.

Hayden, M. (2016). *Playing to the Edge: American Intelligence in the Age of Terror*. New York: Penguin Press.

He, G., Dai, H., and Mao, R. (2013). Homogenization of Provincial TV's International Channels. *Television Research* 8, 38–40 [in Chinese].

Heikkilä, H. and Kunelius, R. (2017). Surveillance and the Structural Transformation of Privacy: Mapping the Conceptual Landscape of Journalism in the post-Snowden Era. *Digital Journalism* (published online: 28 Nov 2016).

Hooghe, L., and Marks, G. (2012). Politicization. In: E. Jones, A. Menon, and S. Weatherill (eds), *The Oxford Handbook of the European Union*. Oxford: Oxford University Press, 841–9.

Jaspers, K. (1954). The Political Vacuum in Germany. *Foreign Affairs* 32(4), 595–607.

Jenkins, H., Ford, S. and Green, J. (2010). *Spreadable Media: Creating Value and Meaning in a Networked Culture*. New York: New York University Press.

Keller, B. (2013). Is Glenn Greenwald the Future of News? *New York Times*, 27 October. Available: http://www.nytimes.com/2013/10/28/opinion/a-conversation-in-lieu-of-a-column.html.

Kleinwächter, W., and Almeida, V. (2015). The Internet Governance Ecosystem and the Rainforest. IEEE Internet Computing. Available: http://ieeexplore.ieee.org/stamp/stamp.jsp?tp=andarnumber=7061808 (accessed Mar. 2016).

Klinger, U., and Svensson, J. (2014). The Emergence of Network Media Logic in Political Communication: A Theoretical Approach. *New Media and Society* 17(2), 151–67.

Lee, M. (2013). Encryption Works: How to Protect Your Privacy in the Age of NSA Surveillance. Freedom of the Press Foundation. https://freedom.press/encryption-works (accessed May 2015).

Lewis, J. (2010). Sovereignty and the Role of Government in Cyberspace. *Brown Journal of World Affairs* 12(2), 55–65.

Lewis, S. (2012). The Tension between Professional Control and Open Participation: Journalism and its Boundaries. *Information, Communication and Society* 15(6), 836–66.

———. (2015). Epilogue. Studying the Boundaries of Journalism: Where do we Go from Here? In: M. Carlson and S. Lewis (eds). *Boundaries of Journalism: Professionalism, Practices and Participation*. New York: Routledge.

Lloyd, J. (2017). *Journalism in an Age of Terror: Covering and Uncovering the Secret State*. London: I.B.Tauris.

Lyon, D. (2007). *Surveillance Studies: An Overview*. Cambridge: Polity.

MacDonald, M., and Hunter, D. (2013). Security, Population and Governmentality: UK Counter-Terrorism Discourse 2007–2011. *Critical Approaches to Discourse Analysis across Disciplines* 6, 2.

MacDonald, M., Hunter, D., and O'Regan, J. (2013). Citizenship, Community, and Counter-Terrorism: UK Security Discourse, 2001–2011. *Journal of Language and Politics* 12(3), 445–73.

McGarrity, N. (2011). Fourth Estate or Government Lapdog? The Role of the Australian Media in the Counter-Terrorism Context. *Continuum: Journal of Media and Cultural Studies* 25(2), 273–83.

Mackenzie, A. (2002). *Transductions: Bodies and Machines at Speed*. London: Continuum.

Malone, G. (1985). Managing Public Diplomacy. *Washington Quarterly* 8 (Summer), 199–213.

Mancini, P. (2005). Is there a European Model of Journalism? In: H. de Burgh (ed.), *Making Journalists: Diverse Models, Global Issues*. London: Routledge, 77–93.

———. (2012). Instrumentalization of the Media vs. Political Parallelism. *Chinese Journal of Communication* 5(3), 262–80.

Mathiesen, T. (2012). Preface. In: C. Fuchs, K. Boersma, A. Albrechtslund, and M. Sandoval (eds), *Internet and Surveillance: The Challenges of Web 2.0 and Social Media*. New York: Routledge, pp. xv–xix.

Min, D. H. (2014). Online Media and Internet Communication in China in 2014. People.cn, 22 December. Retrieved from http://media.people.com.cn/n/2014/1222/c40628-26253298.html [in Chinese].

Mols, A. and Janssen, S. (2017). Not Interesting Enough to be Followed by the NSA: An Analysis of Dutch Privacy Attitudes. *Digital Journalism*. Published online: 5 October 2016.

Morgenthau, H. (2005 [1948]). *Politics among Nations: The Struggle for Power and Peace*. Boston: McGraw-Hill.

Morozov, E. (2013). *To Save Everything, Click Here: Technology, Solutionism, and the Urge to Fix Problems that don't Exist*. New York: Public Affairs.

Mueller, M. (2002). *Ruling the Root: Internet Governance and the Taming of Cyberspace*. Cambridge, MA: MIT Press.

Myers, S., and Leskovec, J. (2014). The Bursty Dynamics of the Twitter Information Network. Proceedings of the 23rd International Conference on World Wide Web. New York: ACM, 913–24.

Nerone, J. (2015a). *The Media and Public Life: A History*. Cambridge: Polity.

———. (2015b). Journalism's Crisis of Hegemony. *Javnost/The Public* 22(4), 313–27.

Neuman, R., Guggenheim, L., Mo Jang, S., and Young Bae, S. (2014). The Dynamics of Public Attention: Agenda-Setting Theory Meets Big Data. *Journal of Communication* 64, 193–214.

Nicolson, H. G. (1963). *Diplomacy*, 3rd edn. London: Oxford University Press.

Nissenbaum, Helen (2010). *Privacy in Context: Technology, Policy, and the Integrity of Social Life*. Palo Alto, CA: Stanford University Press.

Nocetti, J. (2015). Contest and Conquest: Russia and Global Internet Governance. *International Affairs* 91, 111–30.

Nossek, H. (2004). Our News and their News: The Role of National Identity in the Coverage of Foreign News. *Journalism* 5(3), 343–68.

Nye, J. S. (2004). *Soft Power: The Means to Success in International Politics*. New York: Public Affairs.

Oates, S. (2007). The Neo-Soviet Model of the Media. *Europe-Asia Studies* 59(8), 1279–97.

———. (2013). *Revolution Stalled: The Political Limits of the Internet in the Post-Soviet Sphere*. New York: Oxford University Press.

Oliver, R. (2004). *What is Transparency?* New York: McGraw-Hill.

Papacharissi, Z. (2010). Toward a Technography of Cyberspace: An Article Reviewing the Books 'Making Digital Cultures: Access, Interactivity, and Authenticity' by M. Hand, 'The Information Society' by R. Hassan and 'Media, Modernity and Technology: The Geography of the New', by D. Morley. *New Media and Society* 12(3), 515–20.

———. (2015). Toward New Journalism(s): Affective News, Hybridity, and Liminal Spaces. *Journalism Studies* 16(1), 27–40.

Parker, E. (2014). Putin's Cyberphobia. *Foreign Policy*, 24 Sept. http://foreignpolicy.com/articles/2014/09/24/putin_cyberphobia_russia_internet_media (accessed Mar. 2016).

Pei, S., Muchnik, L., Tang, S., Zheng, Z., and Makse, H. (2015). *Exploring the Complex Pattern of Information Spreading in Online Blog Communities*. Plus One Open Access research publisher. doi: 10.1371/journal.pone.0126894 (accessed Mar. 2016).

Picard, R. (2015). The Humanisation of Media? Social Media and the Reformation of Communication. *Communication Research and Practice* 1(1), 32–41.

Plenel, E. (1999). *Les mots volés*. Paris: Folio.

———. (2006). *Le journaliste et le président*. Paris: Stock.

Pontaut, J-M., and Pontaut, J. (1996). *Les oreilles du président*. Paris: Fayard.

Popkin, J. (1989). *Revolutionary News: The Press in France*. Durham, NC: Duke University Press.

Preibusch, S. (2015). Privacy Behaviors After Snowden. *Communications of the ACM* 58(5), 48–55.

Qin, J. (2015). Hero on Twitter, Traitor on News: How Social Media and Legacy News Frame Snowden. *International Journal of Press/Politics* 20-1, 66–184.

Risse, T. (2014). European Public Spheres, the Politicization of EU Affairs, and its Consequences. In: T. Risse (ed.), *European Public Spheres: Politics is Back*. Cambridge: Cambridge University Press, 141–64.

Robinson, P. (2002). *The CNN Effect: The Myth of News Media, Foreign Policy and Intervention*. New York: Routledge.

Rohozinski, R., et al. (2000). How the Internet Did Not Transform Russia. *Current History* 99(639), 334–8.

Roose, J. (2015). Politisiert die Krise? Veränderungen bei der Diskussion EU-politischer Fragen in der Bevölkerung. In: Jörg Rössel and Jochen Roose (eds), *Empirische Kultursoziolgie: Festschrift für Jürgen Gerhards zum 60. Geburtstag*. Wiesbaden: VS Springer, 425–54.

Rosen, J. (2013). Out of the Press Box and into the Field. Pressthink, 17 Nov. http://pressthink.org./

Roudakova, Natalia (2008). Media-Political Clientelism: Lessons from Anthropology. *Media, Culture and Society* 30, 41–59.

Rusbridger, A. (2013). The Snowden Leaks and the Public. *New York Review of Books* 60(18), 31–4, www.nybooks.com/articles/archives/2013/nov/21/snowden-leaks-and-public/?pagination=false (accessed Mar. 2016).

———. (2015). Interview with Risto Kunelius and Adrienne Russell, London, 15 June.

Russell, A. (2016). *Journalism as Activism: Recoding Media Power*. Cambridge: Polity.

Russell, A. and Waisbord, S. (2017). The Snowden Revelations and the Networked Fourth Estate. *International Journal of Communication* 11, 1–22.

Sagar, R. (2013). *Secrets and Leaks: The Dilemma of State Secrecy*. Princeton, NJ: Princeton University Press.

Schell, O. (2004). Preface. In: M. Massig (ed.) *Now They Tell Us*. New York: New York Review of Books.

Schudson, M. (2015). *The Rise of the Right to Know: Politics and the Culture of Transparency, 1945–1975*. Cambridge, MA: Harvard University Press.

Schudson, M., and Anderson, C. (2008). Objectivity, Professionalism, and Truth Seeking in Journalism. In: K. Wahl-Jorgensen and T. Hanitzsch (eds), *Handbook of Journalism Studies*. New York: Routledge, 88–101.

Schulze, M. (2015). Patterns of Surveillance Legitimization: The German Discourse on the NSA Scandal. *Surveillance and Society* 13(2), 197–217.

Seib, P. (2012). *Real-Time Diplomacy: Politics and Power in the Social Media Era*. Basingstoke: Palgrave Macmillan.

Sewell, W. (2005). *The Logic of History: Social Theory and Social Transformation*. Chicago: Chicago University Press.

Simons, G. (2015). Russian Media and Censorship: A Means or an End? *Russian Journal of Communication* 7(3), 300–12.

Soldatov, A., and Borogan, I. (2010). *The New Nobility: The Restoration of Russia's Security State and the Enduring Legacy of the KGB*. New York: Public Affairs.

———. (2013). Russia's Surveillance State. *World Policy Journal* 30(3), 23–30.

———. (2015). *The Red Web: Between Russia's Digital Dictators and the New Online Revolutionaries*. New York: Perseus Books.

Solove, Daniel (2011). *Nothing to Hide: The False Trade-Off between Privacy and Security*. New Haven: Yale University Press.

Stohl, C., Stohl, M., and Leonardi, P. M. (2016). Managing Opacity: Information Visibility and the Paradox of Transparency in the Digital Age. *International Journal of Communication* 10, 123–37.

Thompson, J. (1995). *The Media and Modernity: A Social Theory of the Media*. Cambridge: Polity.

Thussu, D. (2015). Digital BRICS: Building a NWICO 2.0? In: K. Nordenstreng and D. Thussu (eds), *Mapping BRICS Media*. New York: Routledge, 242–63.

Tuch, H. (1990). *Communicating with the World: US Public Diplomacy Overseas*. New York: St Martin's Press.

Tuchman, G. (1973). Making News by Doing Work: Routinizing the Unexpected. *American Journal of Sociology* 79(1), 110–31.

Turner, F. (2006). *From Counterculture to Cyberculture: Stewart Brand, The Whole World Network, and the Rise of Digital Utopianism*. Chicago: Chicago University Press.

Vincent, D. (2016). *Privacy: A Short History*. Cambridge: Polity.

Volkmer, I. (2014). *The Global Public Sphere: Public Communication in the Age of Reflective Interdependence*. Cambridge: Polity Press.

Wahl-Jorgensen, K., Cable, J., Bennett, L., Hintz, A., and Dencik, L. (2015). Hero, Traitor, Whistle-Blower, Spy: An Examination of the British Press' Coverage of State Surveillance and the Edward Snowden Revelations. Future of Journalism Conference, 10–11 Sept., Cardiff University.

Waisbord, S. (2013). *Reinventing Professionalism*. London: Polity.

Wang, H., Lee, F., and Wang, B. (2013). Foreign News as a Marketable Power Display: Foreign Disasters Reporting by the Chinese Local Media. *International Journal of Communication* 7, 884–902.

Weiss, T., and Wilkinson, R. (2014). Rethinking Global Governance? Complexity, Authority, Power, Change. *International Studies Quarterly* 58(1), 207–15.

Wilde, P., de Leupold, A., and Schmidtke, H. (2015). Introduction: The Differentiated Politicisation of European Governance. *West European Politics* 39(1), 3–22.

Wizner, B. (2015a). Keynote Remarks. *Surveillance and Citizenship: State–Media–Citizen Relations After the Snowden Leaks*. Cardiff University, 18–19 June.

———. (2015b). Interview Elisabeth Eide and Risto Kunelius, Cardiff, 18 June.

Wood, D., and Wright, S. (2015). Before and After Snowden. *Surveillance and Society* 13(2), 132–8.

Yuan, S. (2013). *Chinese Journals Going Out: Aiming High But Moving with Burdens*. www.chinaxwcb.com/2013-09/12/content_276968.htm [in Chinese] (accessed Mar. 2016).

Zaller, J., and Chiu, D. (1996). Government's Little Helper: US Press Coverage of Foreign Policy Crises, 1945–1991. *Political Communication* 13, 385–405.

Zheng, Y. (2014). Sino-US Relations and the Future of International Order. *International Politics Research* 1, 36–48.

Zürn, M. (2015). Opening up Europe: Next Steps in Politicisation Research. *West European Politics* 39(1), 164–82.

Index

RISJ/I.B.TAURIS PUBLICATIONS

CHALLENGES

The Right to be Forgotten: Privacy and the Media in the Digital Age
George Brock
ISBN: 978 1 78453 592 6

The Kidnapping of Journalists: Reporting from High-Risk Conflict Zones
Robert G. Picard and Hannah Storm
ISBN: 978 1 78453 589 6

Innovators in Digital News
Lucy Küng
ISBN: 978 1 78453 416 5

Journalism and PR: News Media and Public Relations in the Digital Age
John Lloyd and Laura Toogood
ISBN: 978 1 78453 062 4

Reporting the EU: News, Media and the European Institutions
John Lloyd and Cristina Marconi
ISBN: 978 1 78453 065 5

Women and Journalism
Suzanne Franks
ISBN: 978 1 78076 585 3

Climate Change in the Media: Reporting Risk and Uncertainty
James Painter
ISBN: 978 1 78076 588 4

Transformations in Egyptian Journalism
Naomi Sakr
ISBN: 978 1 78076 589 1

BOOKS

Journalism and the NSA Revelations: Privacy, Security and the Press
Risto Kunelius, Heikki Heikkilä, Adrienne Russell and
Dmitry Yagodin (eds)
ISBN: 978 1 78453 675 6 (HB); 978 1 78453 676 3 (PB)

Journalism in an Age of Terror: Covering and Uncovering the Secret State
John Lloyd
ISBN: 978 1 78453 790 6 (HB); 978 1 78453 708 1 (PB)

Media, Revolution and Politics in Egypt: The Story of an Uprising
Abdalla F. Hassan
ISBN: 978 1 78453 217 8 (HB); 978 1 78453 218 5 (PB)

*The Euro Crisis in the Media: Journalistic Coverage of Economic Crisis and
European Institutions*
Robert G. Picard (ed.)
ISBN: 978 1 78453 059 4 (HB); 978 1 78453 060 0 (PB)

Local Journalism: The Decline of Newspapers and the Rise of Digital Media
Rasmus Kleis Nielsen (ed.)
ISBN: 978 1 78453 320 5 (HB); 978 1 78453 321 2 (PB)

The Ethics of Journalism: Individual, Institutional and Cultural Influences
Wendy N. Wyatt (ed.)
ISBN: 978 1 78076 673 7 (HB); 978 1 78076 674 4 (PB)

*Political Journalism in Transition: Western Europe in a
Comparative Perspective*
Raymond Kuhn and Rasmus Kleis Nielsen (eds)
ISBN: 978 1 78076 677 5 (HB); 978 1 78076 678 2 (PB)

*Transparency in Politics and the Media: Accountability and
Open Government*
Nigel Bowles, James T. Hamilton and David A. L. Levy (eds)
ISBN: 978 1 78076 675 1 (HB); 978 1 78076 676 8 (PB)

Media and Public Shaming: Drawing the Boundaries of Disclosure
Julian Petley (ed.)
ISBN: 978 1 78076 586 0 (HB); 978 1 78076 587 7 (PB)